INTERMEDIATE 1 & 2
History
course notes

× John A Kerr ×

ISBN 9781843728788

Published by
Leckie & Leckie Ltd
An imprint of HarperCollinsPublishers
Westerhill Road, Bishopbriggs, Glasgow, G64 2QT
T: 0844 576 8126   F: 0844 576 8131
leckieandleckie@harpercollins.co.uk   www.leckieandleckie.co.uk

Special thanks to
Helen Bleck (copy-editor)
Jennifer Shaw (proofreader)
Integra-India (creative packaging)

A CIP Catalogue record for this book is available from the British Library.

Acknowledgements
Leckie & Leckie has made every effort to trace all copyright holders.
If any have been inadvertently overlooked, we will be pleased to make the necessary arrangements.

We would like to thank the following for permission to reproduce their material:
CollinsBartholemew for the maps on pages 6–7, 43, 55 and 70–71
Punch Ltd for 'The Goosestep' by Ernest Howard Shepard, originally published in *Punch Magazine*, 18 March 1936 (page 28),
Solo Syndication and the British Cartoon Archive for:
'Increasing Pressure' by David Low, originally published in the *Evening Standard*, 18 February 1938 (page 31);
'What's Czechoslovakia to me, anyway?' by David Low, originally published in the *Evening Standard*, 18 July 1938 (page 33);
'Santa Hitler' (page 34) by David Low, originally published in the *Evening Standard*, 10 October 1938;
'Rendezvous' by David Low, originally published in the *Evening Standard*, 20 September 1939 (page 37);
'Here's to the brave new world!' by Leslie Gilbert Illingworth, originally published in the *Daily Mail*, 2 December 1942 (page 53).

Introduction 4

Iron and Blood? Bismarck and the creation of the German Empire, 1815–71

Part 1	Germany 1815–48	8
Part 2	Germany and the revolutions of 1848	12
Part 3	Bismarck and the unification of Germany	16
Part 4	How important was Bismarck to German unification?	21

The Road to War, 1933–39

Part 1	The beginning of appeasement	24
Part 2	Rearmament and the Rhineland	27
Part 3	Hitler starts to move east	30
Part 4	Czechoslovakia and the Munich Agreement	32
Part 5	The Polish crisis	36
Part 6	Was the policy of appeasement justified in the 1930s?	39

From the Cradle to the Grave? Social Welfare in Britain, 1890s–1951

Part 1	Changing attitudes to poverty and its causes around 1900	44
Part 2	The Liberal reforms, 1906–14	46
Part 3	Labour and the welfare state 1945–51	50

Campaigning for Change: Social Change in Scotland, 1900s–79

Part 1	The changing role of women	56
Part 2	Changes in the Scottish way of life	62
Part 3	Changing patterns of employment	65

Free at Last? Race Relations in the USA, 1918–68

Part 1	The USA in 1918	72
Part 2	Jim Crow and the Ku Klux Klan	78
Part 3	The civil rights campaigns between 1945 and 1965	81
Part 4	Black Radical protest	86

This book will help you gain an Intermediate 1 or 2 qualification in History. It contains what you need to know about five popular topics studied at Intermediate 1 and Intermediate 2.

This book provides all the information you need to answer successfully all the assessments you will face on these five popular topics.

You will be helped to develop skills in explaining historical developments and events. You will also be helped to think about the information you have and to reach conclusions.

In the Intermediate 1 and Intermediate 2 courses, you must choose three topics to study. The full list of topics can be found on the SQA website:

http://www.sqa.org.uk/sqa/files_ccc/History_Int_2_Arrangements_v6.pdf

One of these topics must be chosen from the list of Scottish or British topics.
Your second choice must be from the SQA list of European and world topics.
Your third choice can be from either list.
Each unit includes specific historical themes.

There are two topics from the Scottish or British list dealt with fully in this book:
- From the Cradle to the Grave? Social Welfare in Britain, 1890s–1951
- Campaigning for Change: Social Change in Scotland, 1900s–79

There are three topics from the European and world list dealt with fully in this book:
- Iron and Blood? Bismarck and the Creation of the German Empire, 1815–71
- The Road to War, 1933–39
- Free at Last? Race Relations in the USA, 1918–68

You might also find the following books useful when looking for more information for your extended response. They are also written by John A Kerr and published by Leckie & Leckie.
- *Higher History Course Notes Book 1* (ISBN 9781843726975) – the information on the UK, (suitable for From the Cradle to the Grave? and Campaigning for Change), appeasement (The Road to War) and Germany (Iron and Blood?) is more fully developed in these books
- *Higher History Grade Booster* (ISBN 9781843727293) – the section on the extended essay contains very useful advice about essay writing that could help your Intermediate extended response.

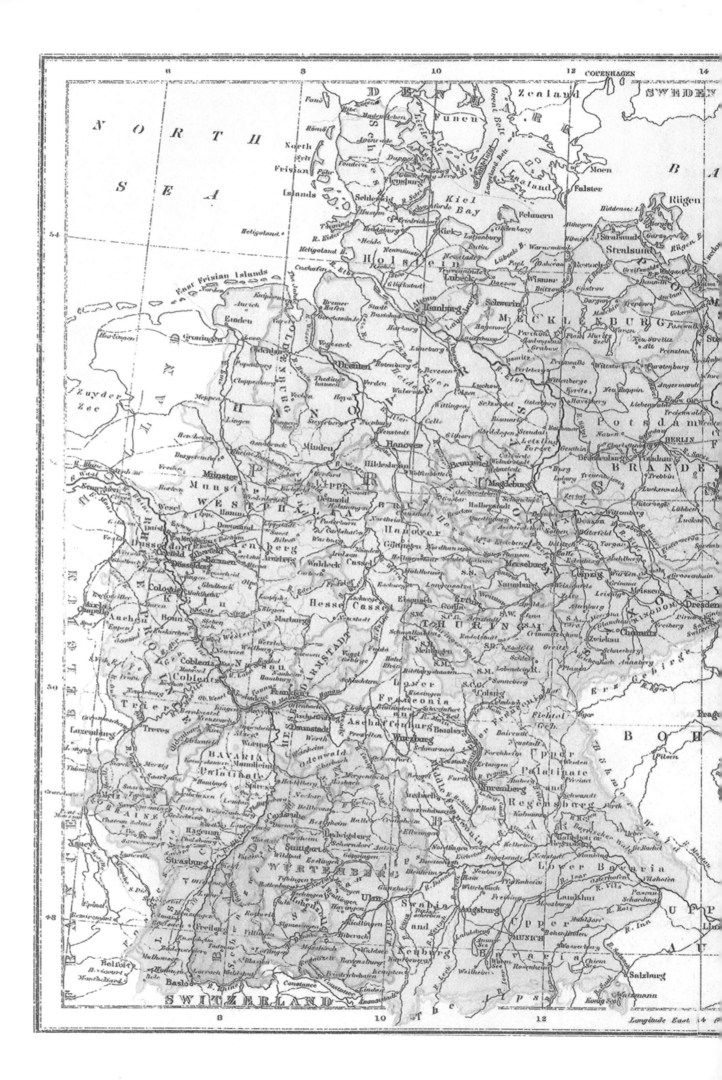

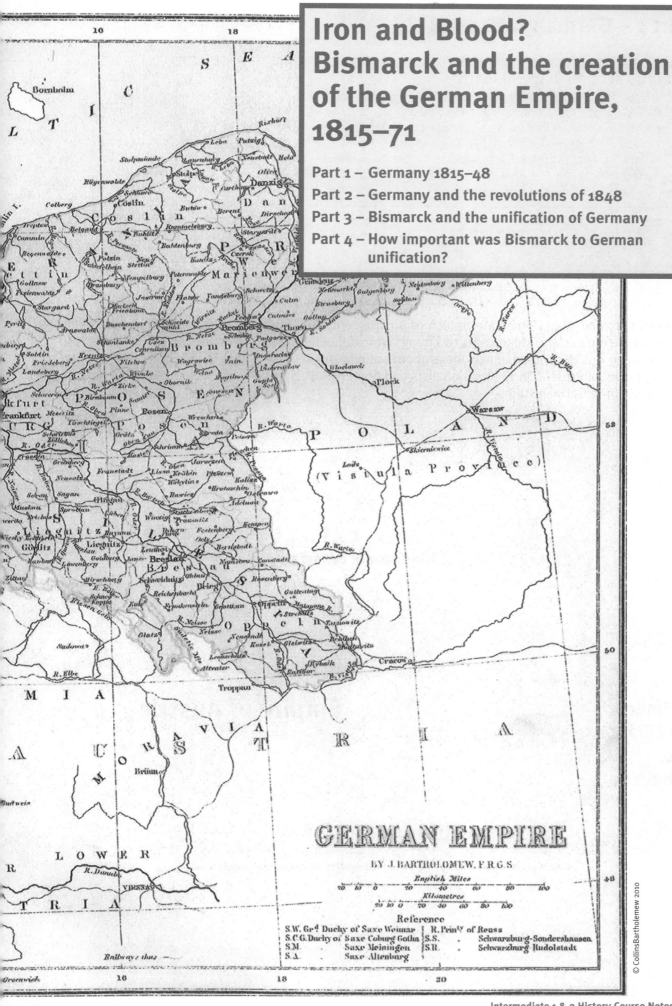

Iron and Blood? Bismarck and the creation of the German Empire, 1815–71

Part 1 – Germany 1815–48

Part 2 – Germany and the revolutions of 1848

Part 3 – Bismarck and the unification of Germany

Part 4 – How important was Bismarck to German unification?

GERMAN EMPIRE

BY J. BARTHOLOMEW, F.R.G.S.

English Miles

Kilometres

Reference

S.W. Gr^d Duchy of Saxe Weimar | R. Prin^{ty} of Reuss
S.C.G. Duchy of Saxe Coburg Gotha | S.S. | Schwarzburg-Sondershausen
S.M. | Saxe Meiningen | S.R. | Schwarzburg Rudolstadt
S.A. | Saxe Altenburg

Part 1 – Germany 1815–48

In this section you will learn:
- How the Vienna Settlement of 1815 affected the German states.
- Why support for German nationalism grew in the early nineteenth century.
- How the state of Prussia became more powerful in the first half of the nineteenth century.
- How the Zollverein increased Prussian strength.
- Why Austria was fearful of changes in the German states.
- The reasons for the growth of German nationalism after 1815 and the start of Austro–Prussian rivalry.

At a glance:
In 1815, Germany did not exist as a single country. Instead, the territory that later became Germany was made up of many separate states ruled by a collection of princes, dukes and other important noblemen. The Austrian empire and its chancellor, Prince Metternich, dominated those states.

Between 1815 and 1848, Prince Metternich of Austria controlled the German states and opposed any change to the old system. Meanwhile, two things were happening that threatened Metternich's control. The first thing was the spread of new ideas about nationalism and liberalism. The second thing was the growing power of Prussia. In 1848 nationalists and liberals hoped that Prussia would challenge Austria for control of the German states.

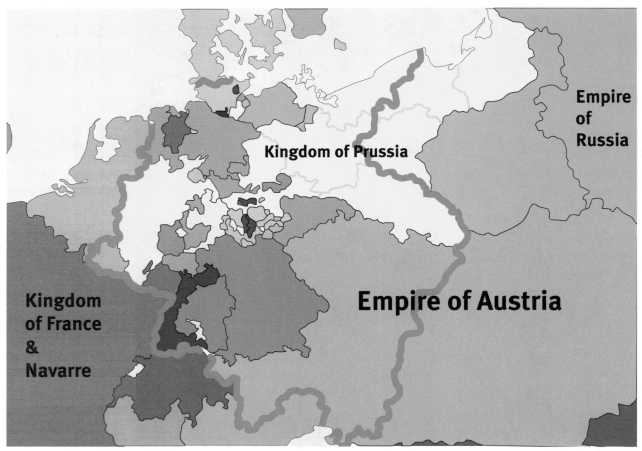

Europe in 1815. The solid red line marks the boundary of the German Confederation.

In what ways did Napoleon's actions before 1815 affect German attitudes?

In his book *Europe since Napoleon,* historian David Thomson wrote that 'the French... spread liberalism by intention but created nationalism by inadvertence'. He meant by this that the French intended to spread new political ideas such as liberalism, but when they defeated and occupied the German states, some Germans started to feel a common identity, or sense of nationhood, because they faced a common enemy – the French.

When Napoleon reorganised the German states (there were originally over four hundred) into thirty-eight bigger states, he only chose sixteen to become the Confederation of the Rhine. Napoleon did not want a united Germany. He was more concerned with protecting France from its enemies. He wanted the River Rhine to be a strong border against France's enemies.

What was the German Confederation?

When the Napoleonic Wars ended in 1815, political leaders from the victorious countries met in Vienna, capital of the Austrian empire. Their job was to restore the power of the former rulers of the German states and Austria.

In the German states, Napoleon's Confederation of the Rhine was replaced by the **German Confederation**, also known as the Bund, or Diet. The German Confederation was mainly a renamed Confederation of the Rhine, with very few changes. It was not a move towards liberalism or national unification.

In fact, the German Confederation was designed to prevent too much change. The German Confederation represented the rulers of the German states, not the people. The rulers in the Diet, and especially Austria, were against any changes that would weaken their authority.

Why did the rulers of the German states and Austria fear nationalism and liberalism?

The largest power in the German confederation was the Austrian empire. In 1815 this empire was the strongest European mainland power, but new ideas such as liberalism and nationalism were threatening its unity.

Nationalism means that people with a common national identity want to have their own country. Nationalism is the belief that belonging to a nation is more important than belonging to a town, class, social group or religious group.

Prince Metternich

Liberalism was the desire to have a parliament where the people of the country elected a government to rule them.

Prince Metternich, who was the Austrian chancellor, hoped to use the German Confederation to stop the spread of nationalist and liberal ideas that could threaten the power of the old rulers.

How did the Vienna Settlement spark off major changes in Germany?

Once Napoleon was defeated in 1815 the leaders of the main European powers met at Vienna to sort out the future of Europe. In fact, the Vienna Settlement sowed the seeds of future conflict between Austria and Prussia.

Metternich believed it was in Austria's interests to keep Germany divided and therefore easier to control. However, at the Vienna meetings in 1815, Prussia was given more land in the centre and west of Germany as a reward for fighting Napoleon. The result was that Prussia became the biggest 'German' state. In hindsight, it is possible to see here the beginning of the rivalry between Austria and Prussia that would not be ended until Prussia defeated Austria in the war of 1866. (See pages 16–18.)

How did Metternich react to growing support for nationalism?

After 1815, Metternich became worried about the growth of student societies, many of which supported liberalism and nationalism. In 1817, the conflict between Metternich and the students reached a peak at a festival in Wartburg, Saxony, when a life-sized model of Metternich was thrown onto a fire. Metternich was furious, and very worried. If nationalist and liberal ideas spread, Austria's power would be weakened. The result was the **Carlsbad Decrees** of 1819, which banned student societies and censored newspapers. The following year, the power of the Diet was increased to stop the spread of new ideas in any of the German states. At the same time, many Germans began to think in a more nationalist way and became more interested in their common culture. This was called cultural nationalism.

Although Metternich had used the Carlsbad Decrees to stop political change, there was little he could do about cultural nationalism.

German poets, authors and composers, for example the Grimm brothers and Beethoven, had begun to encourage feelings of national pride in the German states through their work. Johann Fichte, the head of the University of Berlin from 1810 until his death in 1818, summed up the meaning of cultural nationalism when he described Germany as the Fatherland, in which all people spoke the same language and sang the same songs. He ended by saying that freedom was the right to be German and to sort out one's own problems without interference from foreign powers.

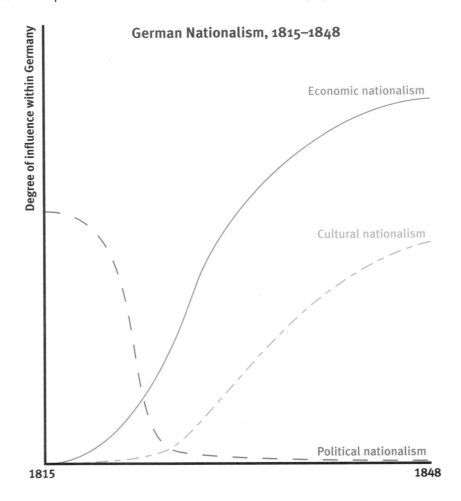

German Nationalism, 1815–1848

Degree of influence within Germany

Economic nationalism

Cultural nationalism

Political nationalism

1815   1848

Why was the Zollverein an important development in the growth of Prussian power?

Although progress towards political nationalism had been seriously slowed down by the Carlsbad Decrees, other changes that would eventually lead to a united Germany were just starting up in the 1820s. These changes can be summed up as economic nationalism.

Prussia had coal and iron, vital ingredients to begin an industrial revolution. As Prussia became richer, smaller states realised they could make money by trading more with Prussia. To encourage trade, Prussia formed a customs union in 1818. This meant that members of the union would not have to pay taxes on goods as they were moved from one member state to another. By the 1830s, this customs union was called the **Zollverein**.

Austria was excluded economically from the German states long before it was excluded politically. Once Austria realised just how important the Zollverein had become it suggested a new organisation called the Zollunion under its own control. However, the plan was rejected by the other German states, who thought that their economic future lay with Prussia.

The Zollverein was an example of economic nationalism because it brought German states together, excluded Austria and increased the power of Prussia.

By 1836, the Zollverein included twenty-five German states, with a total population of 26 million people. The Zollverein did not just help trade, it also helped nationalism to spread. As trade increased, ideas spread and different German states realised that they benefited from closer contact with each other. A new railway network, centred on Prussia, also helped to bring the German states together into a single economic unit.

Why was the Zollverein so important to later unification?

Although the economic changes that the Zollverein encouraged brought the different states together, it was not originally intended to help unification. The separate German states joined the Zollverein for their own financial and economic benefit. The Zollverein did, however, increase the power and status of Prussia and even the Prussian foreign minister had said as early as 1845 that 'unification of states through trade will eventually lead to the creation of a unified political system under our leadership'. Without the Zollverein, Prussia would not have had the muscle to defeat the power of Austria. Historian William Carr has called the Zollverein 'the mighty lever of German unification'.

To summarise, the Zollverein was very important because:
- it was a major reason why Prussia became the most powerful German state;
- as Prussia's economic strength grew, it became a challenger to Austria for influence over the German states;
- it was a prototype example of what would happen later – a united Germany under Prussian control that excluded Austria. The word prototype means a first version of something. The Zollverein was a version of what would later become a united Germany under Prussian control that excluded Austria.

Part 2 – Germany and the revolutions of 1848

In this section you will learn:
- Why 1848 was called the year of revolutions in Germany.
- What the Frankfurt Parliament was and why it failed.
- Why the hopes of nationalists and liberals were raised in 1848 but crushed in 1849.
- How the balance of power between Austria and Prussia changed between 1849 and 1861.

At a glance:
In 1848 there was discontent all over Europe. Bad harvests, unemployment and dislike of old-fashioned rulers caused demonstrations, protests and even revolutions to break out across Europe. In the German states, the revolutions of 1848 were important because they were the first attempt to challenge Austria's power in Germany. A new German parliament was started in Frankfurt, but failed. Austria recovered its power and tried to make sure that Prussia would not challenge Austrian influence again. However, by the late 1850s Austrian power was declining, while Prussia was about to compete for power in Germany once again.

Why did the German revolution seem to be a success at first?

Revolutions occurred in most European countries during 1848. In March of that year, demonstrations took place in Berlin and other German cities. The old rulers seemed to give in quickly to the demands of the nationalists and liberals, especially when they heard that Metternich had fallen from power and had only just escaped with his life from Vienna.

In Prussia, the king, Frederick William IV, tried to stop the demonstrations by force. Eventually he decided to grant the demonstrators what they wanted. Frederick William agreed that a new German parliament called a National Assembly would meet in the city of Frankfurt in May 1848. He also declared that 'Today I have taken the old German colours... Prussia henceforth merges into Germany'. It looked as if the revolutions had been a success and that the liberals and nationalists had gained what they wanted. Germany seemed well on its way to unification.

What did liberals and nationalists want?

Liberal demonstrators wanted:
- freedom of speech
- freedom of the press
- political rights.

In other words, Liberals wanted an elected national parliament and a written constitution. A constitution is a set of rules about how a country should be governed. Nationalist demonstrators agreed with the liberals, but they added something else to the list of demands – the creation of a united country.

Were the revolutions of 1848 a success?

By the summer of 1848 it seemed as if the revolutions had succeeded. In many German states, the old rulers had fallen from power. The German Confederation had crumbled and a new national parliament in Frankfurt had been created. Meanwhile, Austrian power over the German states had lessened with Metternich's fall from power. The Austrian government also had to deal with revolutions within its own empire.

By 1850 it was all different. The national parliament in Frankfurt had collapsed and Germany was not united. King Frederick William IV of Prussia had refused to lead a united Germany and Austria was back in control.

King Frederick William IV of Prussia

Why did the 1848 revolutions fail?

There were three main reasons why the revolutions of 1848 failed.
- The first reason for the failure was the number of different arguments that broke out within the Frankfurt Parliament.
- The second reason was the argument over the future shape of Germany.
- The third reason was because Frederick William IV, King of Prussia, was looking out for himself.

Reason 1

Within the Frankfurt Parliament, the representatives of the middle classes and the working classes argued about how Germany should be governed.

The middle classes were happy enough to get rid of the Old Order, but were not happy when their own property and businesses were threatened by working-class rioters.

On the other hand, the working classes wanted a revolution to improve their living and working conditions. They didn't think those changes were likely in a parliament controlled by the middle classes who were also their employers.

Reason 2

Should the future shape of Germany be Grossdeutsch (including Austria) or Kleindeutsch (excluding Austria)? Many of the southern German states were Catholic and were supporters of Austria. These states did not want to be ruled by Protestant Prussia and so they supported the Grossdeutsch plan that included Austria. Meanwhile, other states, especially those who had benefited from the Zollverein, supported Kleindeutschand and did not want to include Austria.

Kleindeutsch meant a new united Germany would not include Austria.

OR

Grossdeutsch meant a future united Germany would include Austria.

?

Reason 3

In the spring of 1848, Frederick William of Prussia had said he would lead a united Germany. However, in March 1849 he disappointed the hopes of German nationalists when he refused to accept the offer to become King of Germany. Frederick William changed his mind because he was being realistic. He wanted to hold on to his power and he knew the other German princes and kings would never agree to the Prussian king being made into a sort of super-king with power over them.

Frederick William also knew that Austria was recovering its power. By 1849, the Austrian army was ready to crush opposition, bring back the old rulers and restore the Austrian-controlled German Confederation. The Frankfurt Parliament was not strong enough to resist Austria. It had no army to defend itself and if Frederick William led resistance against Austria there was every chance he would lose his power in Prussia. It made more sense for Frederick William to abandon the revolutionaries of 1848 to their fate.

Finally, Frederick William refused to become King of Germany because he was not happy about being offered the crown by ordinary people. At that time many kings, Frederick William included, believed their power came from God, or at least that they were born to rule and were not given a 'crown from the gutter', as Frederick William described it.

Did the failure of the revolution provide any lessons for the future?

By the end of 1849, the Frankfurt Parliament had crumbled, the revolution was left without a leader and the hopes of liberals and nationalists seemed to be dying. However, Frederick William was still ambitious. He liked the idea of leading a united Germany, as long as he was not controlled by a parliament elected by ordinary people. In 1849, he tried to create a different form of united assembly under his authority.

What was the Erfurt Union?

The Erfurt Union was to be an assembly of German princes under Frederick William's control. However, when the Prussian king tried to persuade the other German princes to join the Erfurt Union, they were unwilling to join, for two reasons.

Firstly, the German princes felt they were being bullied by Frederick William into joining the union. Many German princes now supported Austria to protect themselves from the Prussian king's ambition.

Secondly, Austria was determined to destroy the Prussian challenge to its power, and Schwarzenberg, the new chancellor of Austria, said 'we shall not let ourselves be thrown out of Germany'. He also said 'Let Prussia be humiliated and destroyed'.

What was the Humiliation of Olmutz?

The struggle for influence between Prussia and Austria came to a head in 1850. A state called Hesse-Cassel, part of the Erfurt Union, asked for help putting down a small revolution. Austria and Prussia sent troops to help, both claiming their right to do so. For a time it looked as if war would break out between Austria and Prussia. The struggle grew into a showdown over who had power in the German states. At the last minute, Prussia backed down and a meeting was arranged at Olmutz. In later years, the meeting became known as the Humiliation of Olmutz because it appeared to shame Prussia.

When the Prussian and Austrian politicians met at Olmutz, it looked as if Prussia's chance to lead a united Germany was over forever because:
- Prussia had to agree to the cancellation of the Erfurt Union;
- Prussia had to promise never again to challenge Austria's power;
- the old German Confederation was put back in place.

Had the revolutions achieved anything?

Later in this unit, you will discover the importance of Count Otto von Bismarck, who was to become the first chancellor of a unified Germany. Bismarck is often described as the man who united Germany. However, in 1848, Bismarck was opposed to the liberals and nationalists, and saw the failure of the 1848 revolution as a lesson for the future.

Bismarck became convinced that the revolutions of 1848 failed because Prussia did not have the power to defeat Austria. He said that the problem of how to unite the German states would not be solved 'by speeches and majority votes – that was the mistake of 1848 and 1849'. He went on to say

> **'The position of Prussia in Germany will not be determined by its liberalism but by its power.'**

It would also be wrong to see Olmutz as a crushing blow to Prussia. Prussia's political ambitions were put on hold, but its real power, based on its economy and the Zollverein, was left untouched. During the 1850s, Prussian wealth and industrial power continued to grow rapidly.

How were the hopes of German nationalists kept alive during the 1850s?

In 1850, Prussian power seemed to have been destroyed, yet by 1860 Prussia had recovered and Austria had lost some of its influence.

During the 1850s a number of nationalist Prussian lawyers, teachers and businessmen formed a group that campaigned for national unification. It was called the Nationalverein. They said that the German Confederation should be replaced and that it was the duty of every German to support Prussia in order to achieve firm, strong government.

Clearly, hopes for unification under Prussian leadership were still alive in 1859, nine years after the Humiliation of Olmutz. The hopes of nationalists were not dead.

Why was Austrian power weakening in the 1850s?

Austria knew it would have to break up the Zollverein if Prussian economic strength were to be weakened. In 1852, Austria suggested making a new customs union to replace the Zollverein, but the plan collapsed. Austria also lost an important ally. For many years Austria had been friends with Russia, but in 1854 Austria refused to help Russia in a war with Britain and France. Russia was furious, and Austria lost Russia as a friend.

Around the same time, Austria became involved in a war against Italian nationalists supported by the French. Everyone expected the Austrian armies to win easily, but instead Austria was defeated. News reporters at the time described the Austrian army as lurching from disaster to disaster.

By 1860 it was clear that Austria was not as strong as it had been in earlier years. Its army was weak and disorganised, but only Prussia was in a position to challenge Austrian power. The next few years would tell if Prussia could succeed in its challenge.

Part 3 – Bismarck and the unification of Germany

In this section you will learn:
- Why Bismarck's appointment as Minister-President was an important first step in his moves to strengthen Prussia.
- How Bismarck managed to isolate his opponents and manipulate opportunities to his advantage.
- How Bismarck managed to lead Prussia to victory in wars against Denmark, Austria and France.

At a glance:
Before Bismarck began his campaign to unite Germany, he had to make sure of his authority (on behalf of the king) over the Prussian government and its army. Bismarck's political attitudes were shown in the way he dealt with the Prussian parliament, known as the Landtag.

Once Bismarck felt he was politically strong enough, he used a series of wars to increase the power of Prussia. The first war against Denmark tested the newly reformed Prussian army and also manipulated Austria into a difficult position. The second war against Austria removed that country as a serious threat to Prussian power. The third war against France helped to unite all the German states and unite Germany under Prussian leadership.

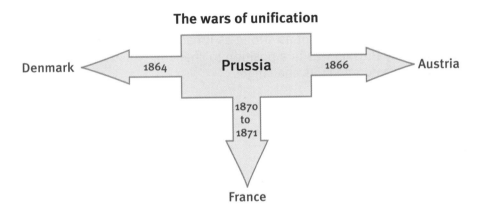

The wars of unification

Denmark ← 1864 — **Prussia** — 1866 → Austria

1870 to 1871

France

Since then, historians have argued over just how much Bismarck planned those wars, or whether if he was just very good at using circumstances to his advantage.

How did a row between the king and Landtag result in Bismarck becoming Minister-President of Prussia?

In 1860, the Prussian Minister of War presented to the Landtag a plan that would restructure the Prussian army and increase its size. However, the liberals in the Landtag objected to this plan, mainly because taxes would have had to be raised to pay for the reforms. The Prussian king, Wilhelm I, was furious, as he believed that the Landtag had no right to block the wishes of his Minister of War. The king even threatened to abdicate, which meant he would resign from his role as ruler of Prussia. However, in September 1862, the king appointed Otto von Bismarck as Minister-President. Bismarck's first job was to sort out the argument over the army reforms.

Bismarck was a supporter of the king, and his solution to the problem was simple – he advised Wilhelm to ignore the Landtag altogether and simply to order the Prussian people to pay the taxes. The army reforms went ahead and when the Landtag protested Bismarck told the king to disband the Landtag altogether.

Bismarck's solution to the row with the Landtag shows clearly his own political ideas. Bismarck believed he was defending the traditional authority of the king against new ideas of liberalism and democracy. Bismarck was loyal to two things – his Prussian homeland and his king.

Otto von Bismarck

What were the 'Wars of Unification'?

Bismarck led Prussia into three wars between 1864 and 1871 which helped to unite Germany. Bismarck's method of unification relied on an efficient army, and in a speech he gave to the Landtag just after his appointment as Minister-President, he made clear how he intended to achieve German unification. He rejected attempts to achieve unification by speeches, discussions and political debates as 'the mistake of 1848 and 1849'. He declared 'the great questions of the day [will] be decided by iron and blood'. He meant unification would be achieved by the use of industrial power and military force.

Why did a war break out between the German Confederation and Denmark?

Bismarck knew the main obstacle to unification would be Austria, but before he could deal with that problem he had to make preparations. Bismarck's first step in weakening Austria's power was a war with Denmark.

In 1863, Christian IX became King of Denmark. Christian wanted more power over Schleswig and Holstein, two areas on the border between Denmark and the German Confederation. Most of the population in Schleswig was Danish, so King Christian used that excuse to claim Schleswig for Denmark, and the Danish parliament passed a new law to absorb the area into the country. Bismarck argued that what Denmark was doing was illegal, and suggested that a combined Prussian and Austrian force should attack Denmark.

Denmark was quickly defeated and Prussia gained the glory as defender of German interests. At the Treaty of Vienna, which marked the end of the war, Denmark gave up its claims to Schleswig and Holstein. However, no agreement was reached about what was to happen to them. At the Convention of Gastein, in August 1865, it was agreed that Holstein would be governed by Austria, and Schleswig by Prussia.

What did Bismarck gain from the conflict with Denmark?

Bismarck knew that if Prussia were to be the most powerful state in Germany, Austrian power would have to be weakened – but not yet.

Bismarck knew the reorganised and modernised Prussian army needed an easy war to test out its organisation and weaponry before it got involved in a war with Austria. A short war with Denmark provided the practice Prussia's military leaders required.

Bismarck's and Prussia's status within the German Confederation were boosted since it looked as if Prussia was a supporter of German nationalism against the threat of Denmark. Meanwhile, Austria could not refuse to get involved in the row with Denmark if it wanted to keep its influence over the German Confederation.

The Convention of Gastein solved nothing. Prussia had control of Schleswig and Austria was left to rule Holstein. To get to Holstein Austria would have to cross through land controlled by Prussia. Austria was politically and militarily cornered. Bismarck could provoke a row with Austria any time he wanted by claiming Austria was not running Holstein properly. In other words, Bismarck could choose when he wanted his showdown with Austria to happen.

The second war of unification – Austria

How did Bismarck prepare for war with Austria?

The first thing Bismarck had to do was isolate Austria. That meant that he had to make sure that no other European power would support Austria against Prussia. Bismarck was worried that if Russia, France or Britain supported Austria then Prussia would not be able to defeat that country.

How did Bismarck make friends with Russia?

Russia was already unhappy about Austria's lack of support ten years earlier when Russia fought Britain and France in the Crimean War. When a nationalist revolt broke out in 1863 in present-day Poland (which was then a part of Russia), Bismarck saw a chance to win Russian friendship. The Polish aim was to break away from Russia and create an independent Poland. Although most of Europe was sympathetic to the Poles, Bismarck stopped Polish refugees escaping into Prussia and so allowed Russia to defeat the Polish revolt easily. By 1865, Bismarck was fairly certain that Russia, formerly a friend of Austria, was now less likely to take sides against Prussia in any future conflict between the two countries.

How did Bismarck make sure that France would not help Austria?

Bismarck knew that there was a possibility that France might help Austria, since both were Catholic countries and suspicious of Prussia. Bismarck had to make sure that France would not get involved in a war between Austria and Prussia.

In October 1865, Bismarck arranged a meeting with the French leader, Napoleon III, at the French seaside resort of Biarritz. Without making any promises, Bismarck hinted very strongly that France would get extra territory, possibly in the Rhineland, if France stayed out of a war between Prussia and Austria. Napoleon III even secretly believed that a war between Prussia and Austria would benefit France, because Prussia and Austria would exhaust themselves in a long war and afterwards France would be left as the strongest power in Europe. All he had to do was wait – or so he thought!

Why did Bismarck make a secret arrangement with Italy?

In the 1860s, Austria controlled most of northern Italy but Bismarck knew that Italian nationalists wanted to break away from Austrian control. He was aware that if he could persuade Italian nationalists to attack from the south while Prussia attacked from the north, then Austria would have to split its armies.

Bismarck suggested a secret alliance between Prussia and Italy. He promised Italy that if it fought for Prussia against Austria then it would be given a reward of land around the city of Venice called Venetia. That land was under the control of Austria and Italians wanted it for themselves. Italy agreed.

By 1866 Bismarck had set the diplomatic scene. He was ready to fight.

How did Bismarck provoke a war with Austria?

Bismarck used the unresolved situation in Schleswig-Holstein caused by the Convention of Gastein to complain that Austria was not running Holstein properly. Bismarck also claimed that Austria was stirring up anti-Prussian feelings in Schleswig. Prussian troops marched into Austrian-controlled Holstein as a punishment. Austria asked states in the German Confederation for support and some of them agreed to take action against Prussia. Bismarck now had what he wanted – an excuse to attack, defeat and take over the smaller German states that supported Austria.

Meanwhile, as part of the agreement between Italy and Prussia, Italy attacked Austria. Austria mobilised all its troops: that meant it was preparing to attack. Bismarck could now claim that he had to take action since Prussia was under direct threat of invasion. In July 1866 Prussia attacked Austria, claiming it was acting in self-defence.

On 3 July 1866 a battle was fought at Königgratz (also called the Battle of Sadowa). The Austrian army suffered a huge defeat with over 40 000 dead, wounded or taken prisoner, compared with a Prussian figure of less than 10 000.

The army reforms that Bismarck had supported now proved their worth. Prussia's military and industrial strength, combined with its efficient railway network, meant that Austria stood little chance. Bismarck's diplomacy before the war also meant that Austria received no help from neighbours. Austria was crushed, and open to Prussian invasion.

Why did Bismarck arrange for a quick and generous peace treaty with Austria?

The Treaty of Prague ended the war between Prussia and Austria and is a good demonstration of **realpolitik**. To Bismarck, realpolitik meant doing what was useful for his future plans. Bismarck did not want to make a long-term enemy of Austria. As a result, the Treaty of Prague treated Austria well. By the end of 1866 the old German Confederation had been abolished and the North German Confederation was created, under Prussian control. The mainly Catholic south German states were grouped into the South German Confederation. Austria lost Venetia, and most importantly Austria had to promise not to become involved in German affairs again.

Bismarck had achieved his aims. He only wanted to weaken Austria's influence over Germany, not to destroy Austria. Bismarck did what was necessary to achieve this aim, and nothing more.

A Kleindeutschland had been created and it seemed as if Germany was close to unity. Prussian liberals were so pleased that most of Germany was united, they forgave Bismarck for the earlier row over army reforms. All that remained was to combine with the south German states and Germany would be united by 'iron and blood'.

Why did Bismarck need to fight a war against France?

In 1866, the southern states of Germany were still outside the North German Confederation. The southern states were mainly Catholic and did not want to be part of the Prussian-dominated North German Confederation. However, Bismarck knew that if France threatened the southern states then the states would look to Prussia for help. Bismarck's problem was that he needed to set up a situation that would make France appear to be in the wrong and a threat to the southern states. Bismarck's chance came when a row broke out over who was to be the next king of Spain.

Historians use the war with France in 1870 as an example of Bismarck taking a situation that was beyond his control and using it to his advantage.

What was the Hohenzollern Candidature?

In 1868, a revolution in Spain led to a search for a new ruler. A distant relative of the Spanish royal family called Leopold of Hohenzollern was found. That meant a member of the Hohenzollern family was a candidate for the Spanish throne – hence the name Hohenzollern Candidature. However, Leopold, as a Hohenzollern, was a member of the Prussian royal family, so France was worried. By looking at a map of Europe you can see that France's southern border is with Spain, and its northern border is mainly with Germany. In 1870 that border land belonged mostly to Prussia. France feared that in any future conflict, it might be trapped between a strong Prussia to the north of France and a Prussian-born king ruling Spain.

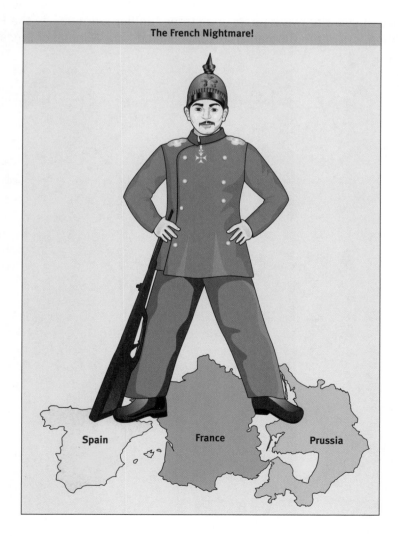

The French Nightmare!

What was the Ems telegram?

The French protested strongly about Leopold becoming King of Spain and even insisted that the Hohenzollern family should give up their claim to the Spanish throne forever. The argument came to a head when the French ambassador, Benedetti, presented the demand directly to King Wilhelm of Prussia while he was on holiday in the resort of Ems.

Wilhelm politely refused and sent a telegram to Bismarck telling him what had happened and how he intended to reply formally to the French.

Bismarck saw his chance and altered the telegram slightly so that it appeared the Prussian king had insulted the French ambassador by refusing to meet him to discuss the Hohenzollern issue.

Bismarck then sent his version of the Ems telegram to the French and German newspapers for publication. The edited version of the telegram had the effect that Bismarck had intended.

The French public were furious at what they saw as the Prussian king's insult to the French. The French emperor, Napoleon III, was still angry at the way he had been tricked by Bismarck over the Austrian war. Napoleon believed that Bismarck had promised him land if he stayed neutral during the Prussian war with Austria but he had got nothing. Now Napoleon III and the French government responded to the anger of the public by declaring war.

Bismarck had gained what he wanted – a war with France which he could claim the French had started!

How did the Franco–Prussian war help to unite Germany?

Within a few weeks of France declaring war in July 1870, the French army was crushed at the Battle of Sedan. The Prussians laid siege to Paris and starved the population of Paris into surrender. France surrendered in January 1871. The North German Confederation and the south German states realised that their only chance of security was as part of a strong, unified Germany. In the Palace of Versailles, just outside Paris, the rulers of the German states proclaimed King Wilhelm of Prussia kaiser (emperor) of a unified Germany.

Part 4 – How important was Bismarck to German unification?

In this section you will learn:
- What the different opinions about Bismarck's importance to German unification are.
- Whether Bismarck had a master plan to unite Germany.
- Whether Bismarck had a real talent to use circumstances to his advantage.
- What Prussianisation meant.

At a glance:
Prussia was victorious in three wars: against Denmark in 1864, Austria in 1866 and France between 1870 and 1871. The result of these wars was an increase in the power of Prussia and the eventual unification of Germany. Ever since, historians have argued over how important Bismarck was to the process of unification.

How important was Bismarck to unification?

There are three main opinions about the importance of Bismarck to unification.
1. Bismarck operated like an architect with a master plan, which he followed in order to build a unified Germany.
2. Bismarck acted as a catalyst to speed up change that would have happened anyway. According to this argument, changes such as the Zollverein, the spread of railways and growing nationalism would have eventually united Germany, even without him.
3. Bismarck had the political skill to take advantage of circumstances as they arose and over which he often had no direct control. Supporters of this view believe he was an opportunist.

Did Bismarck have a master plan?
Be careful if you are arguing that Bismarck had a master plan. Students often refer to a conversation that Bismarck was supposed to have had with a British politician as evidence of a master plan. It is claimed that in the conversation Bismarck outlined how he intended to unite Germany. However, there is no proof that the conversation actually took place.

It is also difficult to decide if Bismarck himself was always telling the truth, especially in his memoirs. In 1890, Bismarck wrote,

> 'I was like a man wandering in a forest. I knew roughly where I was going but I didn't know exactly where I would arrive out of the wood.'

Was he just being modest?

So what is the correct answer to the question 'Did Bismarck have a master plan?' The safest answer, and the one nearest to the truth, is that Bismarck used his talents to strengthen Prussia. The unification of Germany was the outcome of Bismarck increasing the power of Prussia. He was very aware of circumstances, coincidences and other factors that helped him to achieve his aims. Bismarck has been compared to a card player who played his hand very well, even though he did not deal the cards. However, you could say he had a pretty good hand to play!

Was Germany unified or was it Prussianised?
Historians still argue about the word 'unified'. The word suggests that the German states shared a common desire to unite as one country, but many German states were still very suspicious of Prussian power and it looked to them as if Prussia had simply taken over the other states to create a super-Prussia. In fact, the large southern German state of Bavaria was bribed by Bismarck to join the new Germany, and many smaller states believed they had been defeated and absorbed by Prussia rather than choosing to unify.

More evidence to support the idea that the other German states were 'Prussianised' is that the Prussian king became the German kaiser and Bismarck became the German chancellor, while Prussian taxes and laws became German taxes and laws. Such evidence suggests that the German states had been Prussianised rather than unified. Whatever the arguments, however, the fact remains that an independent German empire existed from 1871.

The Road to War, 1933–39

Part 1 – The beginning of appeasement

Part 2 – Rearmament and the Rhineland

Part 3 – Hitler starts to move east

Part 4 – Czechoslovakia and the Munich Agreement

Part 5 – The Polish crisis

Part 6 – Was the policy of appeasement justified in the 1930s?

Sept 3: Britain and France declare war on Germany.

Sept 1: Germany attacks Poland.

March: Germany invades Bohemia and Moravia, parts of Czechoslovakia.

1939

Anschluss – Germany annexes Austria.

Germany takes over the Sudetenland, part of Czechoslovakia.

1938

The Hossbach Memorandum; Hitler makes detailed plans to attack Russia and Eastern Europe.

1937

Nazi warplanes shatter Spanish town of Guernica in Blitzkrieg attack.

Germany remilitarises Rhineland.

1936

Spanish Civil War breaks out.

1935

Germany announces rearmament.

Italy attacks Abyssinia (now Ethiopia).

Germany makes first attempt to take over Austria but fails.

1934

1933

Hitler becomes Chancellor of Germany.

Germany leaves Disarmament Conference and League of Nations after talks freeze.

Disarmament Conference opens in Geneva; US and Soviet Union join League of Nations in talks.

1932

1931 Japan attacks Manchuria in China.

Hitler demands worldwide disarmament, equal to terms Germany met after Treaty of Versailles.

Part 1 – The beginning of appeasement

At a glance:
The Great War was called 'the war to end all wars' because it had killed so many people. Everyone hoped that there would be no more war.

What is appeasement ?

The Treaty of Versailles, signed at the end of World War I, was meant to ensure that Germany never again threatened the peace of Europe. However, by 1933 Hitler and his Nazi party were in power in Germany. One of Hitler's aims was to rip up the Treaty of Versailles. Another was to rebuild the power of Germany. Britain and France were worried about the new threat from Germany, and decided to use a policy of appeasement in their dealings with Hitler. This meant trying to reach agreements with him so as to avoid war.

The aim of appeasement was to remove the possibility of conflict. Appeasement was an attempt to make sure world war never happened again.

When Britain declared war on Germany on 3 September 1939 it seemed that appeasement had failed.

Can the roots of appeasement be traced back to the end of World War I?

The story of appeasement goes back to the end of World War I. At first it was meant to sort out problems arising from the Treaty of Versailles, the peace treaty signed with Germany.

The Treaty of Versailles, signed in June 1919, was very harsh on Germany, which had lost the war. Many Germans did not like the treaty, and one aim of appeasement was to deal with the complaints that Germany had about some parts of it. Tensions created by the treaty were partly responsible for the outbreak of World War II twenty years later.

What happened at the Treaty of Versailles?

In 1919, the victorious allies made Germany sign the Treaty of Versailles.
- Germany was forced to accept blame for causing the war and all the death and destruction that resulted from it. This became known as the War Guilt Clause.
- Germany lost all its colonies, most of its industrial resources and areas of land to neighbouring countries including Poland, France, Belgium and Denmark.
- Germany's armed forces were severely cut. It was not allowed any aircraft, tanks or submarines. Strict limits were placed on the size of its navy. Its army was cut to just 100,000 men.
- Most of the western frontier of Germany, called the Rhineland (including the Saar), was demilitarised, which meant that no German troops were allowed in the area. The intention was to make it impossible for Germany to launch a surprise attack into Belgium and France as it had done in 1914.
- Germany also had to pay reparations (compensation) to the victorious powers.

The Road to War

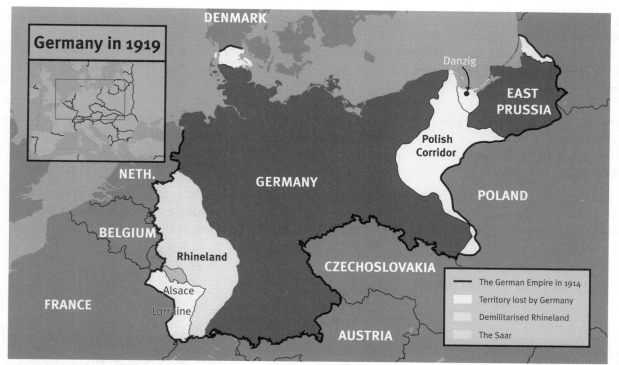

Germany in 1919

	The German Empire in 1914
	Territory lost by Germany
	Demilitarised Rhineland
	The Saar

How Germany was affected by the Treaty of Versailles

How did Germans feel about the Treaty of Versailles?

Most Germans were furious. They called the treaty a Diktat – a dictated treaty that was forced on them. On the same day that the treaty was signed a German newspaper, the 'Deutsche Zeitung', announced

> 'Vengeance, German Nation! Today in the Hall of Mirrors at Versailles, a disgraceful treaty is being signed. Never forget it! Today, German honour is dragged to the grave. Never forget it! The German people will push forward to reconquer their place among the nations of the world. There will be vengeance for the shame of 1919.'

What were the main ideas of Nazi foreign policy in the 1930s?

Much of Nazi foreign policy in the 1930s was based on breaking the Treaty of Versailles in order to re-establish the nation as a strong, influential country.

Adolf Hitler was leader of the Nazi party that came to power in Germany in the early 1930s. One of the reasons why so many Germans supported the Nazis was Hitler's promise to rip up the Treaty of Versailles and make Germany into a powerful nation again.

The policy of appeasement was an attempt by Britain to deal with Hitler's foreign policy.

Hitler's foreign policy was aimed at increasing the size of Germany. It's hard to imagine how he could have achieved his aims without planning for war.

Nearly all of Hitler's actions can be linked to four main aims that he had outlined in his autobiography 'Mein Kampf' ('My Struggle'), written during his time in prison in the mid-1920s.

Adolf Hitler

Aim 1

The Treaty of Versailles had to be destroyed. It symbolised Germany's humiliation. Most of what happened later can be directly linked to Hitler's aim of destroying the Treaty of Versailles.

Aim 2

Hitler wanted all German-speaking people to live in one enlarged Germany. He believed that all Germans had the right to live in Germany, and if that meant that Germany had to take over more land, then he was prepared to make that happen.

Aim 3

Hitler was a racist. He believed Aryans – or Germans – were the Master Race and talked about inferior races such as Jews and Slavs as sub-humans – not even real people. The Nazi word for sub-humans was Untermenschen. Hitler believed the Untermenschen had one purpose in life – to serve the Master Race.

Aim 4

Hitler wanted Germany to have more land and resources. He expected the German population to increase, so he claimed that Germany needed more living space. The German word for that is **Lebensraum**.

Hitler knew that Germany was defeated in World War I partly because it ran out of resources, especially food and oil. He claimed that Germany had to have all the land and resources it needed to survive and grow strong, even if it meant taking these things from other countries. Hitler's ultimate Lebensraum goal was Russia.

These aims can be summed up as:

Hitler's foreign policy aims

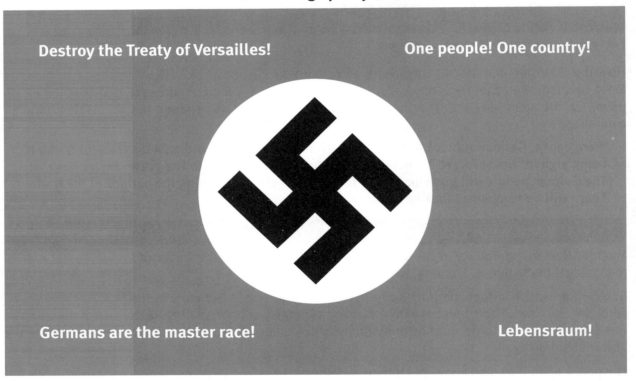

The Road to War

26 | Leckie & Leckie

Part 2 – Rearmament and the Rhineland

> **In this section you will learn:**
> - How Hitler rearmed Germany in 1935.
> - Why Hitler remilitarised the Rhineland in 1936.
> - How Britain reacted to Hitler's actions.

> **At a glance:**
> The Treaty of Versailles ruled that Germany must have no large warships, military aircraft or submarines, but in 1935 Hitler announced his intention to rearm Germany. Rearmament meant that Germany not only increased the size of its army but also the size of its navy and airforce.
> The Treaty of Versailles also banned Germany from having any soldiers in the Rhineland area. In March 1936, Hitler ignored the treaty and sent German soldiers into the Rhineland. Britain and France did nothing to stop him. For several reasons, Britain thought it was best to appease Hitler.

How did Hitler make it difficult for his enemies to stop him?

As you find out more about Hitler's actions in the 1930s, you will discover that he tended to use two tactics to excuse, or justify, his actions.

Hitler's first tactic was to confuse and delay international reaction by claiming that Germany had good reasons for what it did. For example, Hitler justified German rearmament in a speech in 1935 by saying,

> **'In 1919, Germany was disarmed and we were given a promise that other countries would also disarm in a few years. How long do we have to wait? Sixteen years have passed since we were made to disarm. Other countries have done nothing. Today, I say to the world that once again Germany will be strong, but only so that we can defend ourselves and also give our people jobs, making the weapons we need for our defences.'**

Hitler's second tactic was to suggest that if he was allowed just one more change or given one more piece of territory then he would be happy and would make no more demands. This method of increasing Germany's power can be seen in a statement made on the day that he announced German rearmament in March 1935:

> **'I say this to the leaders of Europe. Yes, we are breaking the treaty, but we will get rid of our weapons immediately if other countries do the same. If we are allowed to defend ourselves then we offer a future of peace where all our differences can be discussed peacefully without using force. But if you attack us we will resist to the last man!'**

How did Britain react to German rearmament?

Opinion in Britain was divided about what to do.

On the one hand, some people such as Winston Churchill argued that Hitler was 'moving along the path of war again'.

On the other hand, it can be argued that Britain encouraged further German rearmament when the Anglo–German Naval Treaty was signed in June 1935. In this agreement, Britain accepted the expansion of the German navy, including the use of submarines.

Perhaps British politicians believed it was better for Britain to know how big the German navy was, rather than objecting to rearmament but being in no position to stop it.

By the summer of 1935, Hitler had achieved another aim – to get his enemies to fall out with each other. France was scared of German military growth and made a treaty with Russia. Britain was furious, as it distrusted communist Russia. Meanwhile, France was angered by Britain's naval deal with Germany.

By the end of 1935, Hitler was in a much stronger position. He had once again broken the terms of the Versailles Treaty and got away with it. He had also caused disagreement between Britain and France, the only countries who were a possible concern to Hitler.

What was the remilitarisation of the Rhineland?

The Rhineland is a large area of German land on the border with France and Belgium. The Treaty of Versailles had demilitarised the Rhineland. This meant that no German soldiers were allowed in or near the Rhineland, but the Rhineland remained part of Germany and had **not** been taken away at the Versailles settlement. Hitler did **not** invade the Rhineland. On 7 March 1936, Hitler simply sent German soldiers back into a part of Germany from which they had been banned.

Why did Hitler need to remilitarise the Rhineland?

Hitler knew that remilitarisation broke both the Treaty of Versailles and the Treaty of Locarno, signed in 1926 before he came to power. At Locarno, Germany voluntarily accepted the terms of the Versailles Treaty. However, a demilitarised Rhineland meant that Germany's western border was open to invasion from Hitler's enemies. Before Hitler started his eastward expansion he needed to have a secure and well-defended western frontier.

Why did Britain take no action to stop the remilitarisation of the Rhineland?

Hitler knew he was taking a gamble when he reoccupied the Rhineland.

After World War I a new organisation called the League of Nations had been set up to maintain world peace. The League of Nations had also been set up partly to make sure that the Treaty of Versailles was not broken. Two of the main members of the League of Nations were Britain and France, and they should have taken action against Hitler.

Hitler's military leaders had told him not to remilitarise the Rhineland since the German army was in no position to fight if they had to face any opposition, but Hitler's gamble paid off. Britain and France did nothing to stop the remilitarisation of the Rhineland.

Reason 1
Britain was angered by the French alliance with Russia, signed in 1935. The British felt that Hitler had some justification in claiming that remilitarisation was a defensive move to balance the threat that Germany felt from Russia and France.

Reason 2
By 1936 many people believed that Germany had been treated too severely at Versailles. Lord Lothian, a British politician at the time, summed up the British attitude by saying the Germans were 'only moving troops into their own back garden'. Remember, remilitarisation was not an invasion or an attack against anyone.

Reason 3
Before the remilitarisation, Hitler had said he would sign a twenty-five-year peace agreement with Britain and France if he were allowed to remilitarise the Rhineland. He also suggested he would start to discuss disarmament. Britain hoped that if it appeased Germany over the Rhineland by allowing the remilitarisation, Germany would start talking again about disarmament and promise future peace.

Reason 4
People in Britain did not want another war; there was a very strong anti-war feeling there. Could any politician justify sending British troops to attack Germany when Germany had attacked no other country?

Why did France do nothing about the remilitarisation of the Rhineland?

France would not take action on its own. When France tried to invade part of Germany in 1923 to enforce part of the Treaty of Versailles the rest of Europe criticised France.

France also had serious internal political difficulties at the time. There was even rioting in Paris. France might well have fallen into political chaos if it got involved in a war with Germany.

France believed Germany was stronger than it really was.

France had spent almost its entire military budget on the Maginot Line – a huge line of fortifications, much of it underground. The French felt safe behind their Maginot Line, described by one observer as 'an expensive hidey-hole'. French military planning was defensive, and French military leaders advised no action against Germany.

What were the results of the remilitarisation of the Rhineland?

Hitler effectively locked the door on the western frontier of Germany. He started to build a line of fortifications along the German/French frontier called the Siegfried Line.

The German public and military commanders were happy; Hitler felt politically safe and able to turn his attention to eastward expansion and his policy of Lebensraum.

THE GOOSE-STEP.

"GOOSEY GOOSEY GANDER,
WHITHER DOST THOU WANDER?"
"ONLY THROUGH THE RHINELAND—
PRAY EXCUSE MY BLUNDER!"

This cartoon, called 'The Goose-Step', is one piece of evidence of how some people in Britain felt at the time. the goose represents the German army. Hitler claimed the remilitarisation was no threat to anyone, but the cartoonist shows a heavily armed goose tearing up a peace treaty. The cartoon was published in the British magazine *Punch* in 1936.

Part 3 – Hitler starts to move east

The Road to War

In this section you will learn:
- What Anschluss was.
- Why earlier attempts at Anschluss had failed.
- Why Anschluss was an important part of Hitler's foreign policy.
- Why Britain decided to appease Hitler again.

At a glance:

In March 1938, German troops marched into Austria, in contravention of the terms of the Treaty of Versailles. Britain and France did nothing to help Austria, and chose to appease Hitler instead.

How did Anschluss fit in with Hitler's foreign policy aims?

Hitler wanted to create a 'Greater Germany' by linking German-speaking people together. He wanted to break the Treaty of Versailles and start spreading east as part of his Lebensraum plan. (But be careful – don't think that he wanted Austria as part of Lebensraum. Austria was just a stepping stone to that target.) The Austrian people spoke German, and the Treaty of Versailles had forbidden Anschluss.

What happened when Hitler tried to take over Austria four years earlier, in 1934?

Hitler tried to take over Austria in 1934 but Mussolini, the leader of Italy, warned Hitler not to do that. Mussolini sent his soldiers to the border between Austria and Italy as a clear signal that if German troops invaded Austria then Italian soldiers would enter the country to prevent Hitler from taking it over. Italy was a neighbour of Austria and at that time Mussolini did not like Hitler. By 1938 things had changed. Mussolini and Hitler had become friendlier and italy would no longer protect Austria from Hitler's ambitions. In political terms, the balance of power had changed.

What was the balance of power?

In 1934 Italy was friendly with Britain and France. Germany was still disarmed and was certainly not strong enough to challenge Britain, France and Italy together. By 1938, the balance of power had changed in Germany's favour. Britain and France had shown they would not stand up against Hitler. Germany had rearmed and now Italy had gone over to Germany's side. In 1938 the balance of power was very much against Britain.

How did Hitler prepare for Anschluss in 1938?

Between 1934 and 1938, the Nazis kept up the pressure on Austria, most of which was organised by an Austrian Nazi called Arthur Seyss-Inquart. Seyss-Inquart's task was to prepare for a Nazi takeover.

When Hitler met with the Austrian Chancellor, Kurt von Schuschnigg, in February 1938, he told Schuschnigg that Austria could expect no help from Britain, France or Italy. Schuschnigg was scared and he hoped to drum up international support for Austria. Schuschnigg's big idea was to gain international publicity to support Austrian independence. He planned a plebiscite (a referendum) to ask the Austrian people if they wanted to be German or if they wanted to stay Austrian.

Schuschnigg was gambling that if the Austrians voted to stay separate from Germany, the whole world would know that Hitler had no excuse to invade Austria.

The plebiscite was planned for 13 March, but Hitler ordered Schuschnigg to call it off.

Meanwhile, Neville Chamberlain, the British prime minister, said: 'Why should we mislead small European countries by giving them an assurance of security when any such security can only be a delusion?'

Clearly, Britain had no intention of helping Austria. Schuschnigg realised that he could expect no help from Britain or France so he called off the plebiscite and resigned. On 12 March 1938, German troops marched unopposed into Austria. Within hours, thousands of Austrian people were cheering and welcoming the German soldiers. Anschluss was complete.

How did Britain react to Anschluss?

The terms of the Versailles agreement were perfectly clear – Anschluss was forbidden. However, once again Britain and France did nothing and therefore Austria was annexed and became part of the German Reich (Empire).

On 7 March 1938, Chamberlain said: 'What small country in Europe today, if threatened by a larger one, can safely rely on the League alone to protect it from invasion? There can only be one honest answer, and that is "no one".'

In this quotation, Chamberlain makes it clear that he believed nothing could be done to save Austria from Anschluss.

Most British people believed that Austria was not their problem and that it was too far away to be given any help. Since many Britons felt that Versailles had been too harsh and since Austria shared a similar culture to Germany, they believed that Anschluss was inevitable.

A typical opinion that shows the majority opinion at the time was contained in a letter from Lord Tweedsmuir, Governor General of Canada, to his sister. He wrote,

> **'I do not myself quite see what there is to fuss about. Austria will be much more comfortable under Germany's wing. That should have been done long ago in the Versailles Treaty. Surely the Versailles agreement was the most half-witted thing ever done?'**

On the other hand, anti-appeasers felt that Hitler was a bully who would keep coming back for more unless he was stopped. Politicians such as Winston Churchill, felt that appeasement just encouraged Hitler's aggression. Anshluss helped Hitler gain more resources, factories, men of military age and control over south-eastern Europe. In a speech in the House of Commons on 14 March, Churchill said,

> **'We cannot leave the Austrian question where it is. Austria is a small country brutally struck down. Vienna [the capital of Austria] is the centre of all the countries lying to the south-east of Europe. The mastery of Vienna gives to Nazi Germany control of the whole of south-east Europe by road, river and by rail. What is the effect of this upon the balance of power?'**

However, although Churchill consistently opposed appeasement, he was not prime minister at the time of Anschluss and he had little influence. There were others who shared his opinion, such as the political cartoonist David Low. Try to see some of his cartoons. They attacked appeasement consistently and showed the reality behind Hitler's expansion.

INCREASING PRESSURE.

In this cartoon by David Low, published in the *Evening Standard*, the person carrying the basket of eggs is meant to be Sir Anthony Eden, who was British Foreign Secretary until his resignation on 20 February 1938. Many people in Britain thought that problems in Austria had nothing to do with Britain. Low is trying to warn people that problems in Europe can easily spread across to Britain. Look at where Britain is standing – on the edge of a cliff and about to trip over a rock. All its 'eggs in one basket' (labelled 'British Empire') will smash. Low is trying to show that Britain is directly threatened by Hitler's actions in Europe.

Part 4 – Czechoslovakia and the Munich Agreement

In this section you will learn:

- Why there was a crisis over Czechoslovakia in 1938.
- Why Chamberlain flew three times within two weeks to meet Hitler.
- What the Munich Agreement was.

At a glance:

In the summer of 1938, another international crisis broke out over the Sudetenland. The Sudetenland was part of Czechoslovakia that contained three million German-speaking people. Hitler wanted to take over the Sudetenland and it looked like a war might break out.

At the last minute the crisis seemed to be solved at a meeting between the leaders of Britain, France, Germany and Italy. The meeting was held at Munich in Germany.

Six months later the policy of appeasement was almost dead when Hitler broke the Munich Agreement.

Why was the Sudetenland at the centre of the crisis?

Czechoslovakia was a new country created after World War I. It contained many different nationalities, including three million German speakers who lived in an area called the Sudetenland. Nazi-controlled territory bordered western Czechoslovakia to the north, the west and the south. Hitler's Lebensraum ambitions meant eastward expansion, but Czechoslovakia, with its strong defences, was a barrier to Hitler's plans. If Hitler got control of the Sudetenland, it would be easy to make further advances into Czechoslovakia.

Hitler encouraged the growth of a Sudeten German party led by Konrad Henlein. Hitler told Henlein to provoke trouble in the Sudetenland. By August 1938, both Hitler and Henlein were trying to provoke pro-Nazi demonstrations there. Hitler hoped the Czech police would take strong action against the demonstrators in the Sudetenland. Hitler would then have his excuse to invade, claiming he was protecting the Sudeten Germans from Czech persecution.

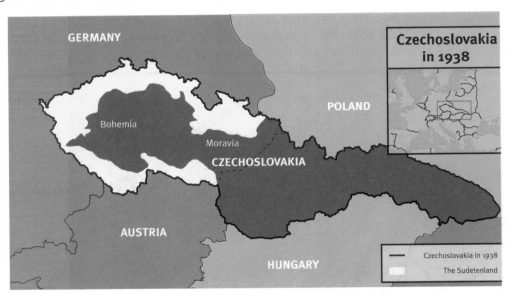

How did Britain react to the growing crisis in the Sudetenland?

By September 1938, Britain was scared. Back in May 1938, Hitler had secretly ordered his army to be ready to attack Czechoslovakia by 1 October. Britain knew about the plan. That deadline was the reason there was such desperate activity in September 1938. The British Prime Minister, Neville Chamberlain, was determined to avoid a war and flew three times to meet Hitler during September 1938. At that time, air travel was still risky and very uncomfortable. Usually political leaders sent representatives to hold meetings that were planned many months in advance. The fact that Chamberlain flew three times within two weeks to meet Hitler face to face shows just how seriously Britain viewed the problem that was growing in the Sudetenland.

The Road to War

Why was Britain involved in the Czech crisis?

Britain was concerned that Czechoslovakia would fight if attacked by Germany. Since France had an alliance with Czechoslovakia, it might fight to help its ally and Britain might also be dragged into the conflict. Britain had no intention of going to war because of France's alliance with Czechoslovakia – and France had no intention of going to war without British support. Britain and France therefore had to find a way to get off the hook.

What happened at the first meeting between Hitler and Chamberlain?

On 15 September 1938 Chamberlain met Hitler at Berchtesgaden, Hitler's holiday home in the mountains of southern Germany. At the meeting, Hitler demanded that the Sudetenland should be given to Germany at some point in the future.

When Chamberlain returned to Britain he persuaded his own government and the French that the agreement should be accepted. It was made clear to the Czechs that if they did not accept the loss of the Sudetenland then they would be left to fight on their own.

Chamberlain was pleased because he seemed to have solved the crisis.

France was relieved because it could now claim it had done its best to secure Czechoslovakia's future. On the other hand, Czechoslovakia was left feeling angry because its ally France had abandoned it and it would be forced to hand over its territory to Germany.

One week later, on 22 September 1938, Chamberlain returned to meet Hitler. This time they met at Bad Godesberg.

Chamberlain went into the meeting confident that the Sudeten problem had been solved. But Hitler had other plans. Hitler was determined to provoke a war, so he demanded that the Sudetenland should be given to Germany immediately. Chamberlain was horrified by Hitler's change of demands.

He returned to Britain expecting war to break out and made a BBC radio broadcast to the British public, saying:

> **'How horrible and unbelievable it is that we should be getting ready for war, trying on gas masks and digging air-raid shelters in Britain because of a faraway quarrel between people of whom we know nothing.'**

It seemed that nothing could prevent war from breaking out. Hitler had demanded a reply from Britain by 2 pm on 28 September but almost at the last minute a new meeting was suggested by Hitler's ally, Mussolini.

Once again, David Low captured not only the attitude of the public, but also the criticism of British policy over Czechoslovakia in one memorable cartoon. The man in the deckchair is meant to be an ordinary British person. Some people in Britain did not see the danger Britain was in. Low shows a rope attached to a rock. When the rock falls so will all the others, and the British person will be crushed. Whose hand is pulling the rope, do you think?

What happened at the Munich Conference?

At the Munich Conference on 29 September 1938, the political leaders of Britain, France, Germany and Italy met to discuss the future of the Sudetenland. Czechoslovakia was not even invited to the meeting, and nor was Russia.

Without consulting Czechoslovakia, it was agreed that Germany would occupy the Sudetenland almost immediately. The Czechoslovakian government was then presented with a choice – either face Germany alone or accept the loss of the Sudetenland. On 30 September, the Czechs accepted the agreement.

Was the Munich Agreement a wise compromise or a betrayal of a friend?

The Munich settlement is still a cause of argument between historians. To some, the carve-up of Czechoslovakia without consulting the Czech representatives seemed a complete betrayal of a good friend. It looked as if Britain and France had given in to Hitler without even trying to stand up to his threats. Churchill, for example, described the Munich settlement as 'an unmitigated defeat'. In a letter to the Scotsman on 1 October 1938 'An Ashamed Peace Lover' wrote,

'I am sure that on hearing the results of the Munich Conference thousands of people will be shocked and humiliated. Britain and France have shown that they are not willing to fight for Czechoslovakia and appear to have thrown Czechoslovakia to the wolves.'

Nevertheless, at the end of September 1938, the majority of the British public was pleased that war had been avoided, at least for the time being.

Britain and Germany both agreed to work to improve relations and to avoid war. Hitler said 'I have no more territorial demands to make in Europe', and Hitler and Chamberlain signed an agreement during their private talk at Munich. When Chamberlain returned to Britain he waved the piece of paper on which the agreement had been signed and which promised 'peace in our time'.

Santa Hitler is taking, not giving! In this cartoon, David Low showed how he felt that the only 'peace' Hitler really offered was under his dictatorship of Europe. Already, Austria and Czechoslovakia are in his bag. The other 'children' of central Europe are crawling towards Hitler, knowing they will be grabbed next and that appeasement will not save them.

Was the Munich Agreement a triumph for the policy of appeasement or a disaster?

Although it is hard now to see Munich as 'peace with honour', as Chamberlain claimed, perhaps it can be seen as a realistic response to the situation at the time. In the 1960s, historian AJP Taylor claimed that the Munich Agreement was a triumph for British policy. He argued that the policy of appeasement was not created to save Austria or Czechoslovakia. It was meant to avoid war through negotiation, and it successfully did that.

In Britain, most people were greatly relieved that war had been avoided. The fear of war, especially gas bombing, was enough to make the public glad that peace had been purchased, even temporarily, at some other country's cost. The Czech crisis was over and the risk of war seemed to have passed. However, events in March 1939 brought Czechoslovakia right back into the headlines.

Part 5 – The Polish crisis

In this section you will learn:
- Why the policy of appeasement was discredited by March 1939.
- Why Poland was Hitler's next target.
- Why war broke out in September 1939.

At a glance:

When Hitler gained the Sudetenland in October 1938, the rest of Czechoslovakia was left defenceless. In March 1939, Hitler tore up the promises made at Munich and invaded the western part of Czechoslovakia. By April, Britain had made promises to protect Poland and Romania, which were Hitler's next likely targets. The promise to protect Poland marked the end of appeasement, and the British government began to prepare an army to fight in Europe.

Hitler believed that Britain's promises meant nothing. However, when Nazi armies invaded Poland in September 1939, Britain declared war on Germany. World War II had started.

Why was the policy of appeasement seen as a failure only six months after the Munich Agreement?

For many people, the settlement of the Czech crisis at Munich suggested that Europe could look forward to a Christmas of peace. In fact, Hitler's promise that he had 'no more territorial demands in Europe' only lasted six months.

Hitler's invasion of western Czechoslovakia (called Bohemia and Moravia – see map on page 32) effectively destroyed any hopes that appeasement might prevent war. Public opinion in Britain and France suddenly changed towards an acceptance that Hitler could only be stopped by force. Even Prime Minister Chamberlain seemed to accept that the policy of appeasement was discredited. In a speech to Parliament at the end of March 1939, he said,

'Have we now to accept that Hitler will not stop and that he cannot be trusted to keep his promises? Must we now face the real possibility that only war will stop the spread of Nazi power? Let me say now that Britain will help Poland if it is attacked by Germany.'

Why was there a Polish crisis in 1939?

Poland was created at the end of World War I, partly out of land taken from Germany and Russia. Look at the map on page 25 to see how Polish land divided the bulk of Germany from a smaller part of Germany called East Prussia. The land belonging to Poland between the two German areas was called the Polish Corridor and contained mostly German-speaking people. Hitler wanted to take over the Polish Corridor. He started his campaign to gain the land by complaining about the treatment of Germans in the Polish Corridor by the Polish authorities.

Why was Russia important to the Polish crisis?

Hitler had gained the Sudetenland fairly easily but he knew the Polish Corridor might be more difficult to win. Britain could do little to help Poland, but next door to Poland was Russia, and Russia was Germany's ultimate target in the east. If Hitler attacked Poland, what would Russia do? Hitler did not yet want a major war with Russia, but would Russia be prepared to fight for Poland?

The leader of Russia, Joseph Stalin, was worried because Russia was not ready to fight. Stalin was also annoyed that he had not been invited to the Munich Conference. It seemed to Stalin that Britain and France were only concerned with protecting themselves, and were not worried if Hitler kept moving east towards Russia. Stalin even suggested an alliance with Britain in April 1939 but Britain rejected the offer. The problem was that Britain was reluctant to make an agreement with communist Russia. Poland, an old enemy of Russia, would not even allow Russian soldiers into Poland – even to help protect it! The result was that by the summer of 1939 no deal between Poland, Britain and

Russia had been made. However, Britain was not too worried. Hitler and Stalin were bitter enemies and Britain knew that any attack on Poland was unlikely, because Hitler did not want to take on the power of Russia.

Why was the world shocked by an agreement between Russia and Germany in August 1939?

The agreement of 23 August 1939 shocked the world because each side was supposed to be the sworn enemy of the other. It was called the Nazi-Soviet Non-Aggression Pact – or sometimes the Molotov–Ribbentrop Agreement after the Russian and German negotiators of the agreement.

The agreement stated that Germany and Russia would not fight each other. There was also a secret part to the agreement. In private, Stalin and Hitler had agreed to divide up Poland between them! The immediate consequence of the agreement was that Germany was free to attack Poland since Russia would not fight to protect it. One week after the Nazi–Soviet agreement was signed, Nazi tanks rolled into Poland on 1 September 1939.

When Hitler invaded Poland, he believed he would have a short, easy war. Russia was now on his side and although Britain had promised to fight for Poland, there was no way Britain could send help across Europe. Hitler was sure that Britain would give in as it always had before, so he was surprised when Chamberlain said that Britain would declare war if German troops did not retreat from Poland.

Last-minute attempts to have a Munich-style meeting failed and Hitler believed he could ignore British threats. On the morning of 3 September 1939 Chamberlain spoke on radio to the British people to tell them that the German invasion of Poland had not stopped and so Britain was at war with Germany.

RENDEZVOUS

This cartoon by David Low, illustrating the dangerous alliance between Hitler and Stalin, was published in the *Evening Standard* on 20 September 1939.

Hitler's gains at the eve of World War II

By September 1939, Hitler's gains were as shown.

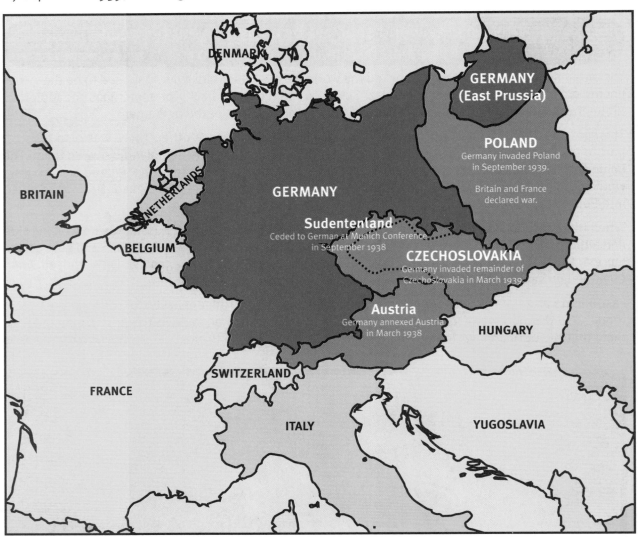

Part 6 – Was the policy of appeasement justified in the 1930s?

> **In this section you will learn:**
> - Why Britain had good reasons to adopt the policy of appeasement in the 1930s.
> - Why the policy of appeasement is still a cause of argument among historians.

> **At a glance:**
> During the 1930s most of the British government and the public seemed to support the policy of appeasement. After the war many historians said that the policy of appeasement had been wrong. All it had done was encourage Hitler's aggression. More recent historians now argue that Neville Chamberlain, British prime minister from 1937 to 1940, had very sensible reasons for using appeasement.

Why did British governments support appeasement in the 1930s?

When explaining why Britain adopted a policy of appeasement you must think of the various pressures that were on the politicians who appeased Hitler.

Strong anti war public opinion in GB

The League was ineffective

Protect the empire

The British Empire might not help

It is not a vital British interest

Rearmament was very expensive

Was France being provocative?

Britain had too many possible enemies

Britain had no allies

The Germans were badly treated after the Great War

Britain had no firm alliance to protect central Europe

The British armed forces were not ready

Hitler was a realistic politician. He would even stop making demands

Political opposition to rearmament

Committee of Imperial Defence said protection of the Empire was Britain's top priority.

Fear of communism

Fear of war

Chiefs of Staff said Britain could not fight a war and win it.

Why did Chamberlain choose appeasement?

Pressure 1
An important reason for adopting appeasement was to avoid war.

Without doubt, the British public in the 1930s wanted peace. The government had to listen to popular opinion since all adults, male and female, now had the right to vote. The public feared a repeat of the previous war and they feared a new war involving gas bombing of cities. In the 1936 movie 'Things to Come', a war starts in 1940 and the film goes on to show British cities destroyed by bombing and the civilian population suffering from gas attacks.

The public had also seen the reality of bombing by watching film of attacks on the Spanish town of Guernica in 1937 during the Spanish Civil War. The town had been utterly destroyed by bombs dropped by Nazi warplanes. It was clear that in any future war the bombing of cities would cause massive loss of life.

Pressure 2

Many people in Britain thought that the Treaty of Versailles had been too hard on Germany. By the mid-1930s, the public and politicians alike believed that some of Hitler's complaints were justified and that Hitler had good reasons for wanting the treaty to be changed. After all, if one part of the treaty could be altered, why not change other parts of it too?

Pressure 3

Some people also believed that Hitler was a reasonable man who could be talked to. Even Chamberlain believed that Hitler was making extreme statements only to gain publicity and that he was essentially a reasonable man who would choose negotiation rather than conflict.

Pressure 4

Britain's number one concern was its empire. A major reason for following a policy of appeasement in Europe was to make sure Britain did not get involved in any European troubles. Any war in Europe involving Britain would threaten the security of its empire. During the 1930s, the British Empire was threatened by Italy and Japan. In 1938 Britain also had to control trouble in India and the Middle East, where 20 000 British troops were trying to keep peace. In short, the empire came first. Appeasement – and keeping out of European conflicts – therefore made sense.

Britain was also concerned that if it got involved in a war in Europe then large parts of the British Empire would think it was nothing to do with them and so would not help. In 1937 the South African prime minister told Britain that, if Britain fought a war over Czechoslovakia, South Africa would not get involved. If that happened, how long would it be before New Zealand, Australia and Canada said a European war was not their problem? Britain would be severely weakened.

Pressure 5

Britain was well aware it had no reliable allies and so war had to be avoided. France was politically split, Italy and Germany were allies with each other and, by late 1939, Russia was allied to Hitler. In 1938, the United States was firmly isolationist. This meant that the USA did not want to get involved in European problems. Chamberlain believed that he could expect no help from America. In a private letter to his sister, he wrote, 'You can count on the Americans for nothing but words.'

The League of Nations had been created to keep the peace and Britain had pinned great hope on its effectiveness. By the mid 1930s the League was effectively dead – what else could keep the peace?

Pressure 6

Britain was also concerned that a war between Hitler's Germany and Britain might lead the way to Communist Russia taking over more territory in Europe.

A common saying at the time was 'better Hitlerism than Communism', and many people wondered what the point of fighting Nazism was, if the result was that Communists came to power in European countries.

Pressure 7

In the 1930s the British economy had problems. Unemployment was high, and the British government wanted to spend money on better housing and welfare for its people. The British government did not want to spend what money it had on expensive weapons. A war would be hugely expensive, so the government hoped appeasement would avoid the need to spend more and more money on rearmament.

Pressure 8

Finally, the heads of Britain's armed forces – the Chiefs of Staff – had consistently warned Chamberlain that Britain was too weak to fight. Britain needed time to rearm. At the same time, Hitler's propaganda encouraged Britain and France to believe that Nazi forces were stronger than they really were.

Would you have supported appeasement in the 1930s?

Even during the 1930s appeasement was controversial. Not everyone supported it, despite what the government and its supporters in the press wanted people to think. Since World War II, the policy of appeasement has been a source of debate among historians. Even today, the policy of appeasement remains controversial.

Given the evidence and arguments you now know about appeasement, would you have supported the policy in the 1930s? Was appeasement a sensible response to the situation confronting Britain in the 1930s? Or do you still think it was a policy of cowardice and foolishness?

From the Cradle to the Grave? Social Welfare in Britain, 1890s–1951

Part 1 – Changing attitudes to poverty and its causes around 1900

Part 2 – The Liberal reforms, 1906–14

Part 3 – Labour and the welfare state, 1945–51

Natural Scale 1: 4,000,000

© CollinsBartholemew 2010

Part 1 – Changing attitudes to poverty and its causes around 1900

In this section you will learn:
- What is meant by self-help and laissez-faire.
- Why attitudes towards poverty were changing in the later nineteenth century.
- What was done to help the poor around 1900.
- How the Booth and Rowntree reports helped to change attitudes towards poverty and its causes.

At a glance:

Laissez-faire is a French phrase that means 'leave alone'. It was used to describe government attitudes to poverty in the nineteenth century. Quite simply, most people accepted that poverty and hardship were not things the government could or should do anything about.

'Self-help' was the idea that people could and should work hard and make sure they did not fall into poverty. The idea of self-help suggested that if people were poor it was their own fault because they were lazy or wasted their money or did not work hard enough.

By the 1890s, many people did not agree with self-help or laissez-faire ideas. Investigations into poverty carried out by two men, Seebohm Rowntree and Charles Booth, proved beyond doubt that poverty had causes way beyond the ability of any individual to solve on their own.

Why did so many people believe in self-help and laissez-faire ideas?

If the government became involved in helping the poor it would cost money. That would mean taxes would have to go up. The wealthy would have to pay more tax so that the government could spend more on helping the poor. An argument used by the wealthier sections of society went like this: 'why should we help people who are too lazy to help themselves?'

Were attitudes towards laissez-faire changing?

During the later nineteenth century attitudes towards laissez-faire were changing. You should be aware that various governments did become much more involved in trying to improve the everyday living and working conditions of the people of Britain. Examples of changing social policy included Factory and Mines Acts that improved working conditions, and Education Acts that made primary education compulsory. The first laws to improve public health were reactions to cholera outbreaks that killed thousands of people. By the end of the nineteenth century there were even attempts to improve slum housing. Therefore, it can be argued that governments were increasingly prepared to become involved in helping to improve the lives of the British people, especially the poor.

What was done to help the poor in the late nineteenth century?

In Scotland, people who were desperately poor and almost starving could go into a poorhouse. In England poorhouses were called workhouses. Some of the poor were given outdoor relief, which meant they could stay at home and be given help. However, the poorhouses were feared and hated by the people who had no choice but to go into them. As a result, many of the poor resorted to begging or depended on charity organisations to help them survive on the streets.

In Victorian Britain, many people felt it was their Christian duty to help the poor. They believed in philanthropy and giving to charity organisations. (Philanthropy means doing things voluntarily to help the less fortunate people in society.)

Recent studies have questioned just how good the local charities were. There was no central organisation at first, so many charity organisations were unsure if they were really helping or not. There was even a fear that some of the poor were getting too much help by asking for help from one organisation after another.

In 1869, the Charity Organisation Society (COS) was set up to manage who got what help, and how much. The COS also had strict rules about who should be helped. They said that the poor should meet all the ordinary expenses of life themselves and not rely on charity. They should work hard and save their money and receive only help in unexpected emergencies. However, it was becoming increasingly clear that the poor could not deal with circumstances beyond their control. Meanwhile, the self-help belief that poverty was in some way the fault of the individual was being questioned more and more.

Why was self-help not always the answer to poverty?

In the 1870s and 1880s there were several years of very high unemployment. Politicians realised that saying that people should just work harder and save more for hard times was not the answer to the huge numbers of poor people on Britain's streets. How could people work harder when there were no jobs available? How could children be blamed for being born into poor families? How could the poor be blamed for being unable to work just because they were too old? By 1900, new research made it clear that poverty was a huge problem in Britain, much bigger than anyone had previously thought.

How important were the reports by Booth and Rowntree in changing attitudes about poverty?

In the late nineteenth century there were two reports into poverty that made people realise that something had to be done about the problem of poverty. The first investigation was into the poor of London and was organised by Charles Booth. The second report was carried out in York and led by Seebohm Rowntree.

At first Booth doubted claims that almost a quarter of the population of London lived in extreme poverty. Booth decided to investigate poverty in the East End of the city. Booth's report eventually filled seventeen large books with hard evidence about the state of London's poor. His report was called *Life and Labour of the People of London*. The evidence collected by Booth and his researchers showed that 35% of London's population lived in extreme poverty, much worse than most people had believed.

The conclusion seemed obvious – poverty was such a big problem that only the government could really help.

Rowntree's investigation into poverty was carried out in York. Rowntree was inspired by the work of Booth in London. Rowntree wanted to find out if London's level of poverty was also common in other places across Britain. Since Rowntree lived and worked in York he decided to find out how big a problem poverty was in that city.

After two years of research, Rowntree published *Poverty, A Study of Town Life* in 1901. Rowntree's report showed that almost 30% of York's population lived in extreme poverty. That meant that the level of poverty in York was almost the same as that found in London by Charles Booth. It was clear from the reports by Booth and Rowntree that poverty was a national problem.

During his research, Rowntree defined poverty very closely. He drew up a 'poverty line' that showed the least amount a family could survive on. Rowntree also defined poverty as either primary or secondary.

If a family suffered from primary poverty, it meant that they could not afford even the bare minimum amount of food, clothing or shelter.

Rowntree defined secondary poverty as the result of earning enough to stay above the poverty line, but then wasting some money on items such as alcohol, gambling or smoking. However, Rowntree knew that such 'wasteful' spending might well be caused by the need to try to escape from the pressures of poverty, even just for a short time.

The reports of Charles Booth and Seebohm Rowntree were important for several reasons.
- First of all, the reports showed that poverty had causes.
- Secondly, the reports showed that no matter how hard certain people tried, they could not lift themselves out of poverty.
- Thirdly, the reports provided evidence that self-help could not cure poverty. Causes of poverty such as old age or unemployment were beyond the ability of an individual to solve on their own.
- Finally, politicians accepted that thousands of people in Britain were poor through no fault of their own and needed help. These people were called the 'deserving poor'. They included children, the old, the sick and the unemployed. Those were the people who were helped by the Liberal Government that came into power in 1906.

Part 2 – The Liberal reforms, 1906–14

In this section you will learn:
- What the Liberal Government did to help the old, the young, the sick and the unemployed.
- How successful the Liberal reforms were in helping to ease the problem of poverty.

At a glance:
Between 1906 and 1914 the Liberal reforms tried to deal with the problem of poverty and focused on four groups: the old, the young, the sick and the unemployed.

The Liberal reforms of 1906–14 were very important because they marked the decline of laissez-faire and self-help ideas. The reforms showed that the government could have a large role in helping those who could not help themselves.

The following diagram should help you organise the basic information about what the Liberals did. The social reforms are organised into four main categories.

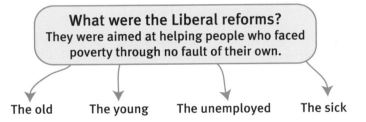

What were the Liberal reforms?
They were aimed at helping people who faced poverty through no fault of their own.

The old   The young   The unemployed   The sick

What was done to help old people?

In 1908 the Old Age Pensions Act was passed in an attempt to help those people who were too old to work and who would slip more and more into complete poverty.

The Liberal politician who did most to start old age pensions was David Lloyd George, the chancellor of the exchequer.

A single person over seventy got a pension of 5 shillings (25 pence) a week, while a married couple got 7 shillings and 6 pence (37·5 pence) each week.

The pension was less for people who earned slightly more than £21 a year. However, those who earned more than £31·50 a year got no pension at all.

There were further conditions attached to pensions: anyone who had been in prison in the previous two years could not claim a pension, and no pension was paid to anyone who had failed to work regularly.

How successful were old age pensions in helping to solve poverty?

Remember, in 1899 Rowntree's study of poverty in York had calculated a poverty line which measured the minimum earnings needed to pay for the barest of necessities. Rowntree calculated the poverty line for an individual to be 35p a week. The full pension was only paid to people who earned less than £21 a year – that's much less than 50p each week.

Clearly, the old age pension came nowhere near meeting all the needs of the elderly poor. Old age pensions helped, but they were not the answer to old age poverty.

Another point to make is that many elderly people needed help long before they reached the age of seventy. Life expectancy for people living in the worst slums was in the mid-forties. By their early fifties most people were too old to continue hard physical work. Critics of the old age pension plan argued that the amount paid was too low and that few of the genuinely poor would live until their seventieth birthday.

Finally, although the amounts of money given as a pension were not enough to prevent poverty, by 1914 there were almost a million elderly people collecting their pension. The Old Age Pension Act may not have solved the problem of poverty for the elderly, but it did make life slightly better.

What was done to help the young?

By the early twentieth century, it was accepted that the deserving poor needed help. The deserving poor were defined as people who were poor through no fault of their own. Clearly, children were a good example of the deserving poor. When the Liberals came into power they passed several reforms to help children.

These reforms dealt with school meals and medical inspections, and created a Children's Charter aimed at child protection.

School meals

By 1906 children had to attend a primary school, but it was well-known that many children were too hungry or too weak to learn. A government report even stated 'It is the height of cruelty to subject half-starved children to the process of education.'

In 1906 the Liberals passed the Provision of School Meals Act. Local authorities were permitted to raise money by increasing rates (a local tax based on property values), but the law did not force local authorities to provide school meals. By 1911, less than a third of all education authorities were using rates to support school meal provision, and almost thirty years later over half of all local authorities were still not providing the service. School meals did make a difference to the children who received them. When children in poor areas were weighed, it was found that they gained weight when they attended school but lost weight again during the holidays when their diet became insufficient for their needs. This suggested that school meals had an important part to play in the health of poor children.

Medical inspections

The Liberal Government knew that poverty and illness were closely connected. They also knew the best way to keep a check on the health of poor children was in school.

In 1907, medical inspections for children were made compulsory. Teachers who felt children were suffering from health problems sent them to the school medical officer, who inspected the children. However, there was no guarantee that each child would be treated. One report stated,

'children suffering from defects likely to affect their education such as problems with sight, uncleanliness, infectious disease and physical weakness are common. However, the local authority inspector only briefly examined the children, he did not provide treatment. Owing to poverty, a large percentage of cases went untreated.'

It was not until free medical treatment for school children began in 1912 that problems could be dealt with.

The Children's Charter

Victorian England was a dangerous place for children. Cruelty to animals was an offence punishable by law, but children had no such protection.

Children were accepted as the group least able to protect themselves from poverty. At the same time, social reformers claimed that poverty was a major factor in starting children out on lives of crime.

The result was that in 1908 a Children's Act was passed which planned to protect children from neglect and abuse. The new law banned children under sixteen from smoking, drinking alcohol or begging. New juvenile courts were set up for children accused of committing crimes. Children found guilty of committing crimes were sent to children's prisons called borstals. It was believed that if young lawbreakers were sent to adult prisons, they would simply learn how to become better criminals. When children were released from borstal, probation officers were employed to help and advise the former offenders in an attempt to stop them reoffending.

All these reforms were called the Children's Charter because it was believed this set of reforms would be like an old-fashioned document or charter which would guarantee better lives for children.

From the Cradle to the Grave?

The Charter contained many new laws; some parts of the Charter were difficult to enforce, while others took time to put into place. The time taken to enforce all the legislation meant the Children's Charter only helped improve conditions for some children during this period, from 1906 to 1914.

How were the unemployed helped?

Both of the reports on poverty written by Rowntree and Booth had identified illness and unemployment as the major causes of poverty. To ease the problem of poverty caused by unemployment or illness, the chancellor of the exchequer, David Lloyd George, introduced a National Insurance Act.

The 1911 National Insurance Act was in two parts. Part one created a scheme of unemployment insurance and a labour exchange scheme. Part two was a health insurance scheme.

The National Insurance Act only covered unemployment for some workers: those in seven particular industries, including construction and shipbuilding. These industries were thought to be most liable to varying employment levels at different times of the year.

In effect, unemployment insurance only covered 2·25 million workers and required contributions from workers, employers and the government. The benefit was 7 shillings a week, paid for a maximum of fifteen weeks. The benefits were paid at the recently opened labour exchanges. At the labour exchanges, which were similar to today's job centres, workers could more easily find out what jobs were available in their area.

Was the scheme helpful?

The help provided by this scheme was useful to workers because it meant they were not immediately without income if they became unemployed. With fifteen weeks to look for work, there was a good chance workers would not face a long time without income. The new labour exchanges also made finding new work much easier.

On the other hand, insurance payments came out of the weekly wage and if a worker suffered long-term unemployment, the benefits would stop being paid after fifteen weeks. In effect, the benefits simply kept an unemployed worker surviving by receiving a poverty-level benefit, and then after fifteen weeks the payment stopped. Since most of Britain's workers were not covered by unemployment insurance they received no help at all.

How did National Insurance aim to help the sick?

In 1911 there was no free National Health Service. The poor could not usually afford medical help, especially as they lost wages during absence from work.

Part two of the National Insurance Act provided medical help for insured workers.

All wage earners between the ages of sixteen and seventy had to join the health scheme. The scheme was called a contributory system, since each worker paid 4p a week towards the help they received. The employer paid 3p a week for each employee and the government paid 2p a week. That meant each insured worker got 9p in benefits from an outlay of 4p. The plan was soon called 'ninepence for fourpence'.

An insured worker got ten shillings (50p) a week for the first thirteen weeks when off sick, but only 5 shillings (25p) a week for the next thirteen weeks. After 26 weeks, the entitlement to benefit ended and the worker was left to seek whatever help he or she could find.

Other help for insured workers was a 30 shillings (£1·50) maternity grant and free medical treatment, including the cost of medicines.

How helpful was the National Insurance Act in helping the sick?

Any money coming in as 'sick pay insurance benefit' would help a family during hard times, but the new law was limited in its help.

- Firstly, only the insured worker got free medical treatment from a doctor. Other family members did not benefit from the scheme, no matter how sick they were.
- Secondly, the scheme did not apply to the self-employed or the slightly better paid.
- Thirdly, the insurance did not cover hospital treatment or treatment by dentists or opticians.

From the Cradle to the Grave?

- Finally, the benefits themselves were very low and payments to the insurance fund reduced the family income. The weekly contributions of 4 pennies had to come out of an already small wage packet that might simply have made poverty worse in many families.

How effective were the Liberal reforms in helping the poor?

The Liberal reforms marked a change in how the government tried to help the poorer sections of the population of Britain.

In the early twentieth century, many people in Britain still sympathised with the idea of self-help as the best way for individuals to escape from poverty. They felt it was wrong for the rich to pay taxes which were used to help people they thought were just lazy. They argued, for example, that old age pensions would stop people saving and encourage them to rely on the government to bail them out when they became poor in old age.

The National Insurance Act is a good illustration of the change in government policy. The government was prepared to intervene to help the poor, but as part of the deal the poor also had to help themselves by paying contributions towards their benefits.

Winston Churchill, who at the time was a Liberal MP, neatly summed up the aim of the Liberal reforms. He said,

'If we see a drowning man we do not drag him to the shore. Instead we provide help to allow him to swim ashore.'

In other words, the Liberals tried to help some of the poorer sections of society to help themselves.

Part 3 – Labour and the welfare state, 1945–51

At a glance:

World War II ended in 1945. In the general election that followed the end of the war, the people of Britain elected a new Labour government. Between 1945 and 1951, the Labour government introduced many social reforms that tried to help improve the lives of the British people. Those social reforms were the foundation of what we now call the welfare state. In a welfare state, the government provides a safety net of support through which no one should fall into poverty. The core idea of the welfare state is that everyone can receive help if and when they need it throughout their life – in other words, 'from the cradle to the grave'.

How did World War II get people in Britain more used to government involvement in their everyday lives?

World War II was important in making people more willing to accept greater government intervention. The phrase 'post-war must be better than pre-war' sums up public attitudes during the war. It meant that people wanted a better Britain after the war and a Ministry of Health statement even said that there could be 'no return to the pre-war position...'

World War II had a big effect on the public's attitude towards the role of the government in their lives. The government organised the rationing of food, clothing and fuel and gave extra milk and meals to expectant mothers and children. Evacuation of poor children from inner-city areas to the suburbs alerted the middle classes of Britain to the real poverty that still existed in the industrial slums. Wartime bombing of cities created vast areas that had to be rebuilt. Free hospital treatment for war wounded – including treatment for civilians with bomb injuries – and free immunisation are examples of the move towards a free health service. And the public got used to higher taxation levels to pay for these services.

Most historians accept that it was the effect of the war that prepared the way for a peacetime welfare state. Many social reforms were either in place or proposed long before Labour swept to power and claimed to establish the welfare state. On the other hand, it was the Labour Government who put the reforms into operation between 1945 and 1951.

How important was the Beveridge Report?

The reforms of the Labour Government were based on five giant problems identified in a report published in 1942. The report was called the Beveridge Report.

The Beveridge Report was published three years before Labour won the election of 1945. The ideas of the Beveridge Report formed the basis of what Labour did after the war to help solve social problems facing Britain.

Beveridge identified five main causes of hardship and poverty. He called them the five giants blocking the path to progress. These giants were:
- want (poverty)
- disease (bad health)
- squalor (bad housing)
- ignorance (poor education)
- idleness (unemployment).

From the Cradle to the Grave?

'From the Cradle to the Grave'

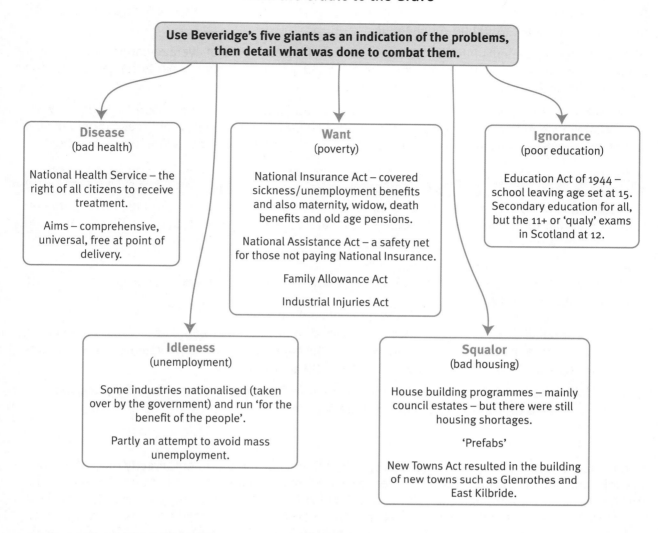

Use Beveridge's five giants as an indication of the problems, then detail what was done to combat them.

Disease
(bad health)

National Health Service – the right of all citizens to receive treatment.

Aims – comprehensive, universal, free at point of delivery.

Want
(poverty)

National Insurance Act – covered sickness/unemployment benefits and also maternity, widow, death benefits and old age pensions.

National Assistance Act – a safety net for those not paying National Insurance.

Family Allowance Act

Industrial Injuries Act

Ignorance
(poor education)

Education Act of 1944 – school leaving age set at 15. Secondary education for all, but the 11+ or 'qualy' exams in Scotland at 12.

Idleness
(unemployment)

Some industries nationalised (taken over by the government) and run 'for the benefit of the people'.

Partly an attempt to avoid mass unemployment.

Squalor
(bad housing)

House building programmes – mainly council estates – but there were still housing shortages.

'Prefabs'

New Towns Act resulted in the building of new towns such as Glenrothes and East Kilbride.

Giant 1 – Want

Beveridge argued that all five of the giant problems he listed in his report had to be defeated if his report were to be successful. However, he knew the biggest giant that affected all the others was **want** – in other words, poverty.

The National Insurance Act of 1946 improved the old Liberal Act of 1911. It allowed for sickness and unemployment benefit, old age pensions for women at sixty and men at sixty-five, widows' and orphans' pensions and maternity and death grants.

All people in work were included in this insurance, but what about those people not in work?

The National Assistance Act helped people who were not in work or the old who had not paid enough contributions into the new National Insurance scheme. People in need could apply for help from National Assistance Boards. Together with the National Insurance Act, National Assistance did provide a safety net through which no person should have fallen into serious poverty. In this case the Labour Government really did try to look after the welfare of the British people from the cradle to the grave.

A Family Allowance Act was also passed to help mothers look after their families if they had two or more children. It was paid at post offices to the mothers because it was believed that if the allowance was paid to men, some would waste the money on drink and gambling. The Family Allowance Act (started by the wartime government) paid 5 shillings a week (25p) for each child in a family apart from the first child, regardless of family income.

Finally, an Industrial Injuries Act paid compensation for all injuries caused at work. The government, not individual employers, paid it. All workers were covered.

How successful were the attacks on want?

By including all workers and families in the benefits scheme, it seemed this attack on poverty caused by shortage of money would be very helpful.

However, weekly payments into the insurance fund took up about 5% of average earnings and people joining the insurance scheme for the first time did not get full pension benefits for ten years. The pensions themselves were still not enough to live on.

Nevertheless, fifty years earlier, Seebohm Rowntree had identified old age, sickness, injury at work and unemployment as the main causes of poverty. Labour had directly attacked these problems and so helped to remove the fear of many people that they might fall into serious long-term poverty.

Giant 2 – Disease

Ill health was both a cause and a result of poverty – but the poor could not afford medical treatment. Labour intended to get around that problem by creating a National Health Service (NHS) that would be free for all to use.

The NHS was based on three main aims.
1. Universal access: the NHS was for everybody. The old health system, based on insurance schemes, did not cover everyone.
2. Comprehensiveness: the NHS would treat all medical problems.
3. Free at point of use: no patient would be asked to pay for any treatment. In reality the service was not free, as the NHS was paid for from the National Insurance payments made by every worker. The point to make is that it for free **at the point of need**.

It entitled everybody, free of charge, to medical care from GPs, specialists and dentists, to spectacles and false teeth and to maternity and child welfare services.

Was the NHS a success?

Before 1948 anyone who received medical care had to pay for the treatment directly out of their own pocket – and pay right away! About half the male workforce was entitled to assistance through various insurance schemes, although their wives and families did not qualify. Many families had no such insurance and in times of illness had to rely for support on friends and neighbours or local charities.

The government inherited many out-of-date hospitals; costs were high and, to keep doctors happy, the NHS operated alongside private medicine. By 1950, the idea of free treatment for all was undermined, but overall the NHS was welcomed and did provide medical help from 'the cradle to the grave'.

The biggest difficulty with the NHS was, and remains, its huge cost. Demand for NHS services surprised everyone. The extent of ill health among the population had not been realised. The running expenses of the NHS were reduced slightly by charging for false teeth, spectacles and prescriptions, but some Labour politicians resigned in protest at this, saying it was breaking the main idea of 'free at the point of need'.

Giant 3 – Squalor

Most of Britain's cities still had slum areas and overcrowding was still a serious problem, made worse by bomb damage during the war. Labour promised homes for everyone and aimed to build 200 000 houses each year. Although only 55 400 new houses were completed in 1946, by 1948 over 280 000 had been built, way above the government's target. Even in 1951 Labour still averaged well over 200 000 houses a year. Most of the new houses were council houses for rent. Many were prefabricated houses – prefabs for short – which were made in factories in sections and quickly assembled on site.

Was Labour's attack on squalor successful?

Many houses were built by 1951 but there was still overcrowding, and long waiting lists for council housing. Cities became encircled with council-owned housing estates providing new, better-quality homes for people moving from the inner cities.

In many ways, council estates were a big improvement on the overcrowded tenements, left behind by the new council tenants. On the plus side, the houses had separate bedrooms, kitchens and living rooms. There was gas and electric power, hot and cold water, indoor toilets in a bathroom, and most houses in the 1950s were two storeys high, usually with gardens at front and back. The downside was summed up by Alex Kerr, who moved from central Edinburgh to an estate in 1953.

> 'I was far away from my work, my friends and the town. The tar was still wet on the roads but there were no shops and no buses at first. We felt lost in the countryside.'

Overall, the new council estates offered a brighter and healthier future for people who had been living in overcrowded tenements in the centre of the cities of Scotland and the rest of the UK. Not least among the advantages was that the rent was now fair and affordable. In the 1950s, council rent was a third of what people had paid to private landlords, who often did not look after their properties well.

Unfortunately, nobody had foreseen the huge demand for housing after the war. Newspaper stories of families squatting in disused army camps while they waited for housing all added to the impression that Labour had failed in its promise. In spite of the huge number of houses built by the Labour Government, there was still a serious housing shortage in 1951 and long waiting lists for council housing.

This cartoon appeared in 1942. The soldier is holding a beer mug with the face of William Beveridge on it! Ten years later, would the soldier feel that Labour's social reforms justified his optimism?

What were new towns?

New towns were deliberate attempts to move town planning away from the chaotic congestion of the older inner cities.

The New Towns Act in 1946 laid the plans for the building of fourteen new towns, including Glenrothes and East Kilbride. Later, more were built, such as Livingston New Town. These were to be 'people-friendly' towns that aimed to relieve the housing problems in older cities.

The housing estates and new towns were also intended to house people 'cleared' from the inner cities, and in turn those inner cities could be redesigned.

In the new towns, traffic was directed away from residential areas, and shopping centres were supplied by purpose-built access roads. Housing estates were centred on medical centres, primary schools and small shops for day-to-day needs.

Giant 4 – Ignorance

Before 1939, many children received no education past primary stage, and poorer parents could not afford the fees that some secondary schools charged. In his report, Beveridge wanted to attack the giant of ignorance by creating an education system available to all, especially the poor, which would provide opportunities and develop talent. During World War II, the wartime coalition planned to reform education. The main idea at the foundations of educational reform was equality of opportunity, which led to the creation of a system that would allow working-class children with ability to gain a good education without having to worry about expensive fees.

The Education Act of 1944 raised the school leaving age to fifteen. All children were to get free secondary education. An exam at the age of eleven (called the 'eleven-plus' exam, or the 'qualy' – short for the Qualification Exam – in Scotland) placed children in certain types of school. Those who passed the exam went to senior secondary schools and were expected to stay on at school after fifteen, go to university and get jobs in management and the professions. Those who failed the exam went to a junior secondary and were not expected to stay at school after the age of fifteen. These children were expected to leave school at fifteen and go into unskilled jobs.

For those who passed the eleven-plus exam, the system worked well. However, those children who failed the exam seemed to be stuck in a trap of low expectations and inferior education. Many people were against the idea of deciding a child's future at the age of eleven or twelve.

Giant 5 – Idleness

In the 1920s and 1930s, unemployment had been very high and, as a result, many thousands of people had been living in poverty. After the war, the Labour Government wanted to avoid high unemployment and aimed ultimately to achieve full employment, which meant that every person who wanted a job could have a job.

Labour's answer to the problem of unemployment was nationalisation. In theory, nationalisation meant that the government would take over major industries and run them for the benefit of the country rather than the private owners. The plan was for the government to control and manage the economy more effectively and maintain full employment. The government could use tax money to keep an industry going even if it was facing economic difficulties. That way people could be kept in work. However, nationalisation was costly and at times led to bad management. The real answer to unemployment was the boom that followed World War II as world trade picked up and American money flooded into Britain. During the 1950s, Harold Macmillan, prime minister of the time, said 'You've never had it so good.' He meant that the British economy was doing well and full employment had been achieved. But this was not really because of nationalisation.

How successful was the Labour Government 1945–51?

The Beveridge Report provided a beacon of hope to war-weary people who wanted to believe that post-war Britain would be a land worth fighting for. Labour's reforms went a long way to creating a post-war Britain based on ideas of fairness and help for all who needed it.

Between 1945 and 1951 the Labour Government tried to create a system known as the welfare state, in which the government looked after the wellbeing of all the people.

The living standards of the poor were raised and people looked forward to a time of increasing opportunity and prosperity. The prosperity and feel-good factor of the 1950s had its roots in the improvements and reforms put into practice by Labour.

By 1951, for the first time ever, the government had removed worries of how to cope with unemployment and serious illness, and a start had been made in providing decent housing and education for everyone. The Labour Government had tried to build a fair society, where help was available to all.

Campaigning for Change: Social Change in Scotland, 1900s–79

Part 1 – The changing role of women
Part 2 – Changes in the Scottish way of life
Part 3 – Changing patterns of employment

© CollinsBartholemew 2010

Part 1 – The changing role of women

In this section you will learn:
- How women campaigned for the right to vote in the early 1900s.
- How the violent campaign of the WSPU affected attitudes towards votes for women.
- How World War I affected women.
- How women were affected by World War II.

At a glance:
By the early 1900s, women were campaigning for the right to vote. One of the largest groups, known as the suffragettes, used violent methods to draw attention to the issue of women's suffrage. Another group, the suffragists, took a more peaceful route. When World War I broke out, women stopped campaigning directly for the vote and many took on men's work for the duration of the war. At the end of the war, some women over the age of thirty were given the right to vote. In 1928, all men and women over the age of twenty one gained the right to vote.

After World War I women returned to traditional 'women's' work but during World War II they once again did vital war work.

Why were so many people against votes for women before 1900?

Traditional views about women in society were slow to change. Many men saw women as irrational, emotional and not suited to politics. Many women were also against the idea of votes for women. It was argued that 'political' women would neglect their feminine duties. Sarah Sewell was one woman who was against women gaining the right to vote and she said,

> **'Educated women rarely make good wives or mothers... nor do they enjoy the interesting work of attending to small children.'**

Even Queen Victoria described the women's suffrage campaign as 'that mad wicked folly of women's rights'. When women's suffrage groups presented petitions to parliament in support of their demands for votes for women, it was quite easy for politicians to ignore them because of the fairly low numbers of signatures.

The following diagram sums up the points you should know about.

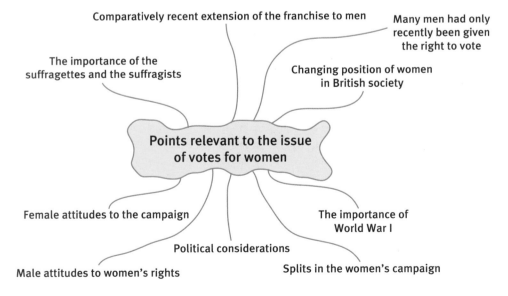

What was the NUWSS, and how important was it to the campaign for votes for women?

In 1897, several local women's suffrage societies united to form the National Union of Women's Suffrage Societies, known as the NUWSS. (The word 'suffrage' means the right to vote.) Members of the NUWSS believed in peaceful methods of campaigning to win the vote, such as writing letters or marching peacefully. Later, the members of the NUWSS were nicknamed the suffragists in contrast to the suffragettes, the popular name for the members of the Women's Social and Political Union (WSPU).

The 'peaceful persuasion' campaign used by the NUWSS has led some people to think that the NUWSS was ineffective, and that the government ignored it. That is not true. The peaceful persuasion tactics of the suffragists did convince many MPs that women deserved the right to vote. It was the suffragettes who lost the support of MPs as a result of their violent protests. Another result of suffragette violence was that many former supporters of the suffragettes switched sides and joined the NUWSS. By 1914 membership of the NUWSS had risen to 53 000 members.

How did the suffragettes campaign for votes for women?

In 1903, Emmeline Pankhurst formed the Women's Social and Political Union. She felt that the peaceful methods of the suffragists were gaining nothing. The WSPU members became known as the suffragettes and at first demonstrated peacefully, with rallies and processions. However, the suffragette campaign soon turned to more violent tactics.

A window-smashing campaign aimed against government buildings started in 1908. In Scotland, the most common form of militant attack was on pillarboxes, where acid was poured in to destroy letters. More suffragette violence followed in 1913, when cricket pavilions, racecourse stands and golf clubhouses were set on fire. In prison the suffragettes kept up pressure on the government by going on hunger strike.

Emmeline Pankhurst – most people associate her with winning the right to vote for women. Others say she pushed back the chances of winning the right to vote.

Hunger strikes were designed to embarrass the government if or when a suffragette died in prison.

The government reacted to the hunger strikers by force-feeding. This meant that hunger strikers would be restrained, their mouths forced open and liquid poured directly into their stomachs. At times, feeding tubes were forced up nostrils if protestors clamped their mouths shut. Serious health complications often arose as a result of force-feeding and the methods used were frequently described as torture.

In response to the bad publicity caused by the force-feeding of hunger strikers, the government introduced a new law. It was nicknamed the Cat and Mouse Act, but its real name was the Prisoner's Temporary Discharge for Ill Health Act. Hunger strikers were left alone until they became ill, then they were released. Once the women had recovered, they were re-arrested, sent back to prison and left there until they completed their sentences. At least, that was the plan! The women who were released did not just wait quietly for the police to re-arrest them. Many women hid and police got bogged down in search and find missions. It seemed that both sides were playing with the other, hence the nickname the Cat and Mouse Act.

When Britain declared war on Germany in August 1914, the government released all suffragette prisoners in exchange for an agreement with the WSPU that they would stop their campaign. The WSPU began a new pro-war propaganda campaign encouraging men to join the armed forces and women to demand 'the right to serve'.

How important were the suffragettes to the campaign for votes for women?

There is great debate among historians regarding the importance of the suffragettes.

Suffragette methods did make big headlines and their actions kept the issue of women's suffrage in the news. However, violent protests by the suffragettes lost public support. The violent protests also lost the support of MPs who had previously supported votes for women. The government was determined not to give in to violent protest methods.

By the summer of 1914, over 1000 suffragettes were in prison and very few people attended public meetings supporting suffragettes. Suffragette membership fell, while the membership of the NUWSS increased between 1910 and 1914.

When the suffragette campaign ended in 1914, women had still not won the right to vote. They had to wait another four years before any woman got the right to vote in a national election.

How did World War I affect the lives and work of women in Scotland?

The Great War is often seen as a major turning point in the role of women in British society. The war opened up jobs to women that would otherwise have been closed to them, and in 1918 some women were given the vote in national elections for the first time.

As casualty rates increased on the battlefield and men were conscripted into the armed forces, women were needed to fill the gaps in the work force left by men who went off to fight.

Elsie Inglis

Industries that had previously excluded women now accepted them. Women worked as conductors on trams and buses, as typists and secretaries in offices and factories, and nearly 200 000 women found work in government departments. Thousands worked on farms in the Land Army, at the docks and even in the police. Some women filled more traditional jobs and during the war nurses such as Elsie Inglis became important role models for women eager to feel they were doing their bit for the war effort.

The biggest increase in female employment was in the engineering industry. Before the war fewer than 4000 women worked in heavy industry in Scotland. During the war over 700 000 women were employed making munitions. Munitions were every type of explosive artillery shell or bullet made for the war effort.

The munitions factories were dangerous places, not just from the risk of explosions but also because of the dangerous chemicals used to make the munitions and explosives.

How did men react to women doing 'their' jobs?

Before the war engineering was a male-dominated industry. When women starting working in the engineering works, men were worried that that their work skills and their wages would be 'diluted'. They felt that the use of women who were trained in the different processes of a job but not to the level of a 'skilled man' would dilute the value of those skilled, trained men. Men feared their status and wages, as skilled men, would be threatened by women doing 'their' jobs.

Women and the rent strikes

The rent strikes of 1915 became an example of how people could take action to fight against unfairness. More importantly, the rent strikes became an example of how women could campaign for change and succeed!

What was a rent strike?

During World War I, the population of the Glasgow area increased as people arrived to meet the demand for workers. Those new arrivals all needed somewhere to stay, and as a result demand for housing in and around Glasgow rocketed – and so did the rents that landlords charged.

There was a strong feeling that the landlords were taking advantage of the women while their menfolk were away fighting in the war. Landlords bullied and threatened the women to make them pay higher rents. Faced with rising food prices and rising rents, some women decided to fight back.

In February 1915 Helen Crawfurd, Mary Barbour, Agnes Dollan and Jessie Stephens helped to form the Glasgow Women's Housing Association to resist the threatened rent rises and possible evictions.

In May 1915 the first rent strike began and soon about 25 000 tenants in Glasgow had joined the strike. The government was under pressure. The rent strikes had grown to the extent that they threatened wartime production of necessary machines and munitions. Men in the engineering factories went on strike to support the women.

The government's answer was the Rent Restriction Act. Rents were frozen at 1914 levels unless improvements had been made to the property. The women's demands had been met and the strikers had learned an important lesson: direct action could lead to positive results.

Please tack this to Top of Lower Sash of Window

Glasgow Labour Party Housing Association

RENT STRIKE
AGAINST INCREASES
WE ARE
NOT REMOVING

Did women gain the vote because of their war work?

One traditional explanation for the granting of the vote to some women in 1918 is that the vote was almost a 'thank you' for their efforts. Is there evidence to support that view?

Remember that the women who worked long hours and risked their lives in munition factories were mostly single, and in their late teens or early twenties. However, the women who were given the vote were 'respectable' ladies with university degrees over thirty years old. They also had to be property owners or married to property owners. These older women were unlikely to have been the ones working as nurses or 'munitionettes', as the workers in the explosives factories were called.

Perhaps a better explanation is that the government was afraid that if nothing was done to give women the vote then the suffragette campaign of violence would start again. In 1918 the recent Russian Revolution had made governments across Europe worried about any social disorder. Could the government be sure that a fresh WSPU campaign after the war would not lead to more suffragette 'terrorism'?

Did the war really change the image and status of working women?

When the war ended, the majority of women did not keep their new-found wartime jobs. A new law called the Restoration of Pre-War Practices Act meant that returning soldiers were given back their jobs. The closure of most munition factories meant that women workers there were no longer needed. Women were forced to leave the men's jobs which they had done during the war years. The idea that a woman's place was in the home was as strong as it had ever been. The marriage bar was also enforced. This meant that a woman had to give up her job the moment she married.

Within a few years of the end of the war, over 25% of all working women were back in domestic service – child-minding and doing housework. That total was higher than before the war.

Did World War II bring about more changes in the role of women?

Before the war, a woman's place was in the home, a man's place was out at work. Nearly five million British women had paid jobs but most expected to leave their jobs as soon as they married, or when they had their first child.

When war broke out, everything changed. With the men away in the armed forces, women not only ran their homes but got used to going out to work as well. Many young, single women had their first taste of living away from home, miles from their parents. Women got used to flexible working hours, nurseries and other arrangements needed to allow women with children to work for the war effort.

War, women and conscription

During World War I, women had volunteered for jobs, and when it became obvious that war was approaching once more, poster campaigns encouraged women to volunteer once again. However, the government was aware that this time the conscription of both men and women would be needed to fight the war.

From spring 1941, every woman in Britain aged eighteen to sixty had to register for service and choose from a range of jobs, although it was made clear that women would not be required to use weapons or fight. The conscription of women began in December 1941. At first, only single women aged twenty to thirty were called up, but by mid-1943, almost all single women and the vast majority of married women were employed in war work.

War, women and work

Most women who volunteered before the war went into civil defence or the Women's Land Army. The main civil defence services were Air Raid Precautions (ARP), the fire service and Women's Voluntary Services (WVS). Typical WVS work included organising evacuations and bomb shelters, clothing exchanges and staffing mobile canteens.

The Women's Land Army/Scottish Land Army was reformed in 1938 so that women could be trained in agricultural work, leaving male workers free to go to war. Women of the Scottish Land Army and Scottish schoolchildren helped to bring in the harvest and potato crop.

Women also supported the army, navy and air force by working in the auxiliary forces. The Auxiliary Territorial Service (ATS) was formed in 1938 to provide driving, clerical and general support in the army. Most of the women in the ATS served in anti-aircraft command, operating searchlights and anti-aircraft guns. The Women's Royal Naval Service (WRNS) was reformed in the spring of 1939 while the Women's Auxiliary Air Force (WAAF) was created in July 1939.

Before long, women made up one third of the total workforce in the metal and chemical industries, as well as in shipbuilding and vehicle manufacture. Women also worked in factories, often in large numbers. For example, 10 000 women worked at the Rolls-Royce factory at Hillington, Ayrshire, making the engines that powered Spitfires and Lancaster bombers.

War, women and fashion

Women's fashion was also affected by the war. Women often wore trousers, or a one-piece siren suit (so-called because it could be pulled on quickly when an air raid warning siren sounded). Headscarves were commonly used as a way of keeping hair out of the way. Large handbags – to carry all the family's ration books – were also practical, rather than just fashionable accessories.

War, women and sex

Social customs also changed hugely. Young women and men had far more opportunities to be alone together. Two results of that were an increase in sexually transmitted diseases and a large increase in the number of babies born to single mothers.

Did greater opportunities for women continue after the war?

During the war, recruitment posters had shown women working for the war effort as glamorous and independent. Images of women, especially those in uniform, were used to sell everything from cigarettes to shoes. Women's contributions to the war effort were highlighted in newspapers and magazines, and women's auxiliary forces paraded regularly through towns. However, when the war ended in 1945, newspapers and films created a new image for women. It was made clear that they were expected to give up their independence and return to the home. Many women were dismissed from their work once peace was declared. Government policy encouraged men to return to their pre-war occupations, and wartime nurseries were wound up. In some industries some women were kept on, but really only because they were cheaper to employ than men.

Part 2 – Changes in the Scottish way of life

In this section you will learn:
- How education changed between the 1920s and the 1940s.
- How people spent their leisure time in the 1920s and 1930s.
- How the Scottish way of life was affected by the arrival of mass entertainment such as cinema and radio.

At a glance:
By the end of World War I, Scotland had become an urbanised society. That meant that most Scots lived in towns. The old way of life based around living in small towns and villages was dying out. In the cities people could be more anonymous. The power of tradition and old customs was becoming weaker. People looked for new forms of entertainment. Meanwhile, the government knew that Scotland's children would have to be educated for a new and changing world.

Why had the government become so involved in education by 1900?

Most scottish children were educated in schools provided by the government. In 1918 local authority education committees took over the running of schools, including those Roman Catholic schools that were now funded by the state. In 1901, the school leaving age was set at fourteen. The leaving age went up to fifteen in 1945.

The public saw education as valuable because:
- schools were places where children could be cared for, for example, with school meals and medical inspections which started in the early 1900s.
- a good education was seen as a way of getting a better job and earning more money. That was especially true for people who had moved into the towns and wanted a better life for their children.

In poorer families there was always pressure for a child to leave school and get a job to bring money into the family. Many state-run secondary schools also charged fees, so not many working-class children stayed on at school or went to university.

In 1914, only 4% of Scotland's children completed secondary education and only 2% went on to university. In 1939, the figures were much the same.

During World War II, the government planned to reform education. The main idea at the basis of educational reform was equality of opportunity, and this meant creating a system that would allow working-class children with ability to gain a good education without having to worry about expensive fees.

The Education Act of 1944 raised the school leaving age to fifteen. All children were to get free secondary education. An exam for all eleven year olds (called the eleven-plus exam, or the 'qualy' – short for the qualification exam – in Scotland) placed children in certain types of school. The system worked well for those who passed their exams. They went to senior secondary schools and were expected to stay on at school after they turned fifteen, go to university and get jobs in management and the professions. However, those children who failed the exam seemed to be stuck in a trap of low expectations and inferior education. These children were expected to leave school at fifteen and go into unskilled jobs. To many people it seemed unfair to decide a child's future at eleven or twelve.

Were there big changes in how Scots spent their leisure time in the 1920s and 1930s?

In the 1920s and 1930s, people living in Scotland's cities had more choice about how to spend their leisure time than ever before.

In 1900 most Scots found their future husbands or wives either in their local village or at church activities. By 1939 partners for life were often found in the dance halls of the cities. Technological advances in transport and entertainment created new patterns of behaviour. By the 1930s, cars, radio and cinema were widening the horizons of urban Scots. People could travel further and do many more different things in their leisure time.

How did most Scots spend their leisure time in the 1920s and 1930s?

Many Scots did much the same sort of thing as they do now – going to cinemas, drinking alcohol, gambling, playing and watching football and enjoying 'street life' in general. 'Street life' was an escape from the overcrowded houses that most urban Scots lived in. For men, pubs offered company, warmth and escape from the home. Football matches offered an exciting escape and, in an urban population that had broken away from its traditional roots, supporting a team gave people a new identity and sense of group belonging. Gambling offered some excitement and maybe, just maybe, the chance of escaping poverty, if only for a short time.

For women, life revolved mainly around their home and family duties. The play 'The Steamie' by Tony Roper, although set after 1939, is a good example of urban Scottish women combining work with some leisure – even if it was just a gossip with neighbours.

How common were drinking and gambling in early 1900s Scotland?

Alcohol was a major social problem. Some reformers hoped that temperance societies, in which people were encouraged to reject all alcohol, were the answer. For children, the Band of Hope and even the Boys Brigade, founded in 1883, offered an alternative way of life avoiding 'the demon drink'. Members of temperance societies were asked to take 'the pledge', which was a promise not to drink alcohol. After World War I some local authorities went completely 'dry', which meant that no alcohol was sold. Most of these areas were 'wet' again by the 1930s, but pubs still closed at 10 p.m. and didn't open at all on Sundays until well into the 1970s.

Gambling was another social problem. In urbanised Scotland, mass entertainment had become a large, commercial and profitable business by the early twentieth century. For most working-class, urban Scots, leisure sports meant football, greyhound racing and horse racing. All of these activities were linked to gambling.

Gambling was believed to be a trap in which the poor stayed poor by risking what little money they had. However, anti-gambling campaigners missed the point that gambling was also a source of excitement and offered at least the possibility of escape from poverty. Local authorities tried to stop gambling by passing laws that stopped 'bookies' taking bets, and the police were given the job of stopping illegal gambling. However, the increasing popularity of respectable and legal gambling such as the football pools made attempts to stop other means of gambling difficult to enforce.

How did mass entertainment change and grow by the 1940s?

By the beginning of the twentieth century, most workers had a half-day holiday, usually on a Saturday. That is one explanation for the very high attendance at football matches that in turn allowed many clubs to turn professional in the late 1800s.

In 1938, all workers were given one week's holiday with pay – by law. This meant that workers could afford to travel further by bus, steamer or railway 'doon the watter' on the west coast, or to the new seaside resorts of Dunbar and North Berwick on the east.

Local authorities tried to provide leisure facilities for urban Scots. Libraries, bandstands in public parks, museums and art galleries still exist in our cities. Most were built in the late nineteenth century.

Many Scots wanted more exciting entertainment. By the 1920s, commercial, large-scale entertainment meant music halls, theatres, dance halls and, by the early 1920s, cinemas. Urban Scotland provided a ready audience for escapism, either in the cinema or the football stadiums.

Did mass entertainment destroy Scottish identity?

In the 1880s, most rural Scots spoke in ways that sounded different from people just a few miles away. They had strong local dialects. Scots living away from the cities also tended to make their own entertainment. There was no opportunity to hear any voice from outside their area unless they met a visitor or travelled themselves.

By 1939, it was harder to define what Scottish culture was. Although radios were still not cheap, they marked the beginning of a world in which every house could hear voices from around the world. Radios spoke to Scots in 'proper' English from the only radio station available – the BBC.

In theatres and music halls they laughed as comedian Harry Lauder made gentle fun of old-fashioned versions of Scottish identity. In the cinemas, Scots were exposed to the values and fashions of the Hollywood 'dream factories'. In dance halls, Scots danced to the latest American jazz and big band music.

It has been argued that the last strongholds of urban Scottish identity were the pubs, the football terraces and the dog tracks. In the isolated rural areas, still not connected to electricity in 1939, an older Scotland lived on until the arrival of television in the 1950s.

Part 3 – Changing patterns of employment

In this section you will learn:
- How Scotland's old traditional industries faced difficulties before and after World War I.
- What 'Red Clydeside' means.
- Why so many workers became disillusioned in the post-war years.
- Why Scotland did not benefit much from the growth of 'new industries' in the 1920s and 1930s.
- How Scotland's older industries still faced problems in the 1960s and 1970s.
- How North Sea oil raised hopes for a boom in Scotland's economy.

At a glance:
Scotland's old traditional heavy industries were facing problems before World War I, and they continued to face serious problems right through into the 1970s. The two world wars temporarily boosted them, but unemployment remained a problem during the inter-war period and also in the 1970s. New industries gave some hope to Scotland's economy and the development of North Sea oil in the 1970s brought prosperity to parts of Scotland.

Why was Scotland called the 'workshop of the world' before 1914?

In 1914, Scotland led the world in the production of coal, iron and steel and in shipbuilding and engineering. Between 1880 and 1914, coal was Scotland's fastest growing industry and in 1900 over 150 000 miners worked in Scotland's coalmines. Just before World War I almost 20% of the world's shipping was built on the Clyde, and Scottish steel towns were producing over a million tonnes of steel each year. In Dundee over seventy jute mills employed tens of thousands of people, especially women.

Were there problems with Scotland's economy before 1914?

There were signs that all was not well with the Scottish economy before 1914.

Scotland relied too heavily on a handful of main 'heavy industries': coalmining, iron and steel making, shipbuilding and engineering. These heavy industries employed most of Scotland's workforce: for example, 14% of the adult male working population of Scotland depended in some way on the shipbuilding industry for their weekly wages.

Even before the war, there was a lack of new investment in Scottish industries. In the case of coalmining, new industries such as oil, gas production and electricity cut demand for coal in people's homes. Foreign competition took away markets and coalmine owners were slow to invest in new, more efficient technology.

The Scottish economy relied on overseas markets. International trade was vital to the Scottish economy. By 1914 it was clear that the world was buying less from Scotland. If trade was disrupted and export markets were lost, the Scottish economy would suffer. For example, shipbuilding depended heavily on international trade, carrying Scottish exports around the world.

Each of the heavy industries was dependant on the other's success. That was one of the causes of Scotland's difficulties after World War I. Less demand for ships would mean less demand for shipbuilders, less demand for iron and steel and less demand for coal!

How did World War I affect Scotland's industries?

At first the war provided a temporary boost for Scotland's industries.

Coal, shipbuilding and the production of iron and steel were all in big demand during the war. However, the demand for production during the war years made the post-war fall in demand much worse.

The introduction of new technology and production methods such as automatic machinery and assembly line production methods speeded up production during the war but also threatened jobs.

After the war, the slump in international trade, the fall in orders for new ships and the use of new production methods all combined to put more people out of work.

Why could Scotland not benefit from new industries?

The real problem was that Scotland relied too much on old industries that had grown up around the raw materials of coal and iron. By the end of World War I, it was clear that new industries were becoming very important, especially in electronics, radio, car and aircraft production and the chemical industry. The problem for Scotland was that these new industries did not need to be based around raw materials. They also developed in the south of England, so did little to help employment in Scotland. Even during the war, workers in Scotland's old industries feared for their jobs, and that led to the rise of 'Red Clydeside'.

Why did the 'Red Clydeside' protests start?

In 1915, disputes broke out between the government and the workers in the engineering factories around the River Clyde. The disputes involved skilled men who had served long apprenticeships and expected to have good pay and a job for life. When war broke out, these skilled men saw their jobs under threat from new machinery, new working methods and also from the use of women in the workforce. The core of the argument was based around the idea of 'dilution'.

What was dilution?
Dilution meant the use of unskilled workers to do parts of a job that had previously been done only by skilled men. In other words, the skill was being lessened – or diluted – by the use of unskilled labour, usually women.

Why did tension increase between the government and the workers on Clydeside?
The government was worried when strikes broke out around the Clyde engineering works in February 1915. The government needed to keep up the production of munitions for the war effort. Meanwhile, the workers were angry with a new law called the Munitions Act, which made strikes illegal.

The rent strikes were also part of the tension and discontent that rumbled through Clydeside in 1915. When the workers in munitions factories went on strike in support of the women organising the rent strikes, the striking men realised the power they had. They felt that any united action that threatened the flow of munitions would make the government sit up and take notice of their demands.

The workers around the Clyde set up the Clyde Workers' Committee (CWC) to organise resistance to government plans. From the government's point of view, the CWC was a nest of revolutionaries ready to upset the war effort and even lead revolution in Britain.

Did strikers on 'Red Clydeside' gain much public sympathy?
Most public opinion supported the government. Newspapers described the strikers as being greedy and selfish. Most public opinion saw the strikers as damaging the chances of winning the war and even endangering the lives of soldiers at the front by trying to limit the supply of munitions.

Why did more 'Red Clydeside' protests break out at the end of the war?
When the war ended, industrial workers across Britain began to fear for their jobs.

They realised that the war had given only a temporary boost to industries that had been facing problems before the war. As munition factories were closed and orders from the government for the machines of war dried up, industrial workers also faced competition for jobs from thousands of returning soldiers.

On Clydeside the CWC was leading a campaign to reduce the working week of fifty-four hours to forty hours, partly to help create jobs for soldiers returning from the war.

Most returning soldiers and workers were disillusioned. They had hoped for homes and work for returning heroes, but instead many saw only unemployment and the same bad living conditions in which they had always lived.

What was the George Square Riot?

A large demonstration to support the cut in working hours and get more jobs for returning soldiers was planned for Friday, 31 January 1919. It was to be held in George Square, Glasgow. As the crowds grew to almost 90 000, clashes between the police and protesters broke out. The government feared that the crowd could easily become a revolutionary mob. Some reports said a red flag was seen flying over the crowd. (The revolutionary flags that were used during the Russian Revolution in 1917 were all red, so the nickname of 'red' for 'revolutionary' stuck.) It was only fourteen months since the Russian Revolution, and in that same month a

German Revolution had occurred. The government clearly felt it had to take action to stop a revolution starting in Scotland. Over 12 000 English troops were brought in by the government to restore order, along with six tanks.

Within a week of the battle at George Square, a forty-seven-hour working week was agreed. The strike was over and 'Red Clydeside' had not sparked off a revolution. Instead, the workers and soldiers who had won the war for Britain returned to a Scotland changing for the worse and heading towards mass unemployment.

Why was there mass unemployment after World War I?

The roots of the problem go back at least to the end of World War I. The problems were worst in the old, traditional industries of steel, shipbuilding, textiles and coalmining. The depressed areas were the places in Britain where the old traditional heavy industries were located, such as central Scotland, the north of England and south Wales.

The British economy faced serious problems after World War I:
- World War I had almost bankrupted Britain. Markets were lost and assets were sold off. In 1919, Britain was poorer and weaker than it had been in 1914.
- By 1920, foreign competition was growing and damaging Britain's trade.
- Britain's policy of free trade allowed foreign goods to enter the country easily, but Britain's competitors often blocked British goods from getting into their countries.
- The decline in British exports hit the old traditional industries. Fewer ships were needed for trading, which meant less iron and steel was needed, which in turn cut demand for coal.
- British businesses became less competitive and less productive, partly because they were slow to invest in new methods and machinery.

Many economists and politicians believed in the cyclical theory of unemployment that meant that there were always short periods of unemployment but that things would pick up again. However, the problems faced by Britain after World War I were structural. This means that British industry had serious problems that would prevent it from recovering. The difficulties in the economy would not automatically recover and unemployment in most of Scotland just got worse throughout the 1920s and 1930s.

Was Britain divided into two nations between World War I and World War II?

On the other hand, for people who had jobs, the 1930s were a time of prosperity and rising living standards. Be careful not to generalise by saying that **all** of Britain in the 1930s was a nation in depression. You must show you are aware that while the older industrial areas in the north of England and central Scotland suffered high unemployment, new industries in the south of England were doing well, and so were the people who lived there.

For those in work during the 1930s the standard of living did get better. For example, a boom in private house-building helped the construction industry. There was also a growth in the consumer industries such as those making motorcars, radios and electrical goods. In other words, Britain could be described as a country of two nations – the depressed areas and the prosperous ones.

In 1900 a report into poverty, called the Rowntree Report, was published. In 1936, a new Rowntree Report looked at how much poverty and living conditions had changed since 1900. The new Rowntree Report found that:

- average family sizes were falling.
- real wages were rising, so people were better off if they had a job. 'Real' wages means what your wages can buy, rather than just looking at the amount of money earned. In the 1930s, prices were falling, which meant that wages bought more!
- a main reason for improvement was the 'remarkable growth in social services during the period'.

However – for many people the 1930s remained a time of mass unemployment and consequently a time of great poverty.

What happened to the Scottish economy in the 1960s and 1970s?

In the late 1960s economic difficulties hit Britain. Scotland's traditional industries continued to decline, and unemployment started to rise again. The problems of Scotland's heavy industries had been obvious since before World War I. In the 1930s Scotland suffered from very high unemployment. However, World War II had given a boost to all of Scotland's industries. In the post-war boom years of the 1950s, a new generation grew up who had never known the depressed years of the 1930s. Tens of thousands of Scots continued to work mining coal, building ships and making iron and steel. The comedian Billy Connolly describes how he was a shipyard worker when he left school and, if he left a job at lunchtime, he could have a new job in the afternoon. Jobs were easy to get and workers thought they were fixed for life.

However, by the 1970s the old problems had reappeared. Foreign competition and lack of investment hit the old heavy industries again; unemployment grew again.

No longer did heavy industry have to be based near the coalfields of central Scotland.

Newer industries such as electronics, making household consumer goods, light engineering and car manufacturing all established themselves in the Midlands and south of England. These industries were nearer better transport links and the mass markets of the south of England and Europe.

In Scotland the government tried to encourage new industries to set up in areas that were declining and where unemployment was high. Car-making factories started production with government help at Linwood and Bathgate. Paper-making and aluminium production were boosted at Fort William. Steel works at Ravenscraig and developments at Hunterston were signs of the 'brave new Scotland'. Government offices were directed north, such as National Savings to Glasgow and Inland Revenue to East Kilbride.

In the 1970s a new development seemed to offer a bright future for Scotland – North Sea oil. Oil and gas were discovered under the North Sea in the late 1950s and the first gas came ashore in 1967. Oil was pumped ashore in the late 1970s. The oil industry created thousands of jobs. Oil rig-making helped shipbuilding yards that were in decline.

Towns in the north-east of Scotland that had been losing population started to prosper again. Before the oil boom Peterhead had a population of 14 000, a top-security prison, some ship repairing and a fishing industry. Unemployment was high. Many people left the area looking for work.

Oil and gas changed all that. Peterhead harbour grew and became a supply base for oil rigs and pipe laying barges. A new tanker terminal was built. Big oil companies set up and Peterhead became a boom town.

By 1979, oil and gas were flowing into Scotland and some parts of the older industries were being helped, such as shipbuilders who converted to oil rig construction and repair. However, the late 1970s also saw an outbreak of strikes, with workers trying to retain their jobs. The discovery of North Sea oil did give a boost to Scotland, but perhaps only disguised the long-term decline of the old heavy industries.

By the end of the 1970s, the older industries were still in decline, and even the newer industries such as car-making brought to Scotland in the 1960s were facing problems. The government pumped money into industries that were clearly in difficulties, just to keep people in work.

There were hopes that new jobs in the service sector and in finance would bring new prosperity to Scotland. Parts of central Scotland became known as Silicon Glen as new electronic and computer companies were attracted to Scotland. However, it was not clear how those highly skilled jobs based in smaller companies could provide work for the thousands of Scots facing unemployment as the shipyards, iron and steel works and the coalmines started to close forever.

Conclusion

Scotland changed a great deal between 1900 and 1979.

This section is called **Campaigning for Change**. That title suggests that many Scots wanted change and campaigned hard to achieve changes in their working conditions and way of life. However, other changes were not so welcome. These changes were forced upon Scotland by influences such as foreign competition or the growth of new forms of mass entertainment.

In 1900, Scotland's people and its industry seemed secure within the British Empire. Glasgow was called the second most important city in the empire. But there were already problems before World War I. Scottish industry faced competition from abroad, and many Scots emigrated to find new lives for themselves in other countries.

In the interwar years, the problems that were hidden before 1914 became more serious. In those years the old secure Scotland with its own recognisable identity began to change. New forms of entertainment, more leisure time and new opportunities to travel by air and car gave Scots new horizons. Social change meant women had greater freedom, and in the 1950s it did look as if a new, prosperous Scotland would rebuild itself.

However, in the 1960s and 1970s the problems of the older declining industries became more obvious. Unemployment began to creep up again and the hopes for new industries such as North Sea oil did not offer permanent solutions to Scotland's economic and social difficulties.

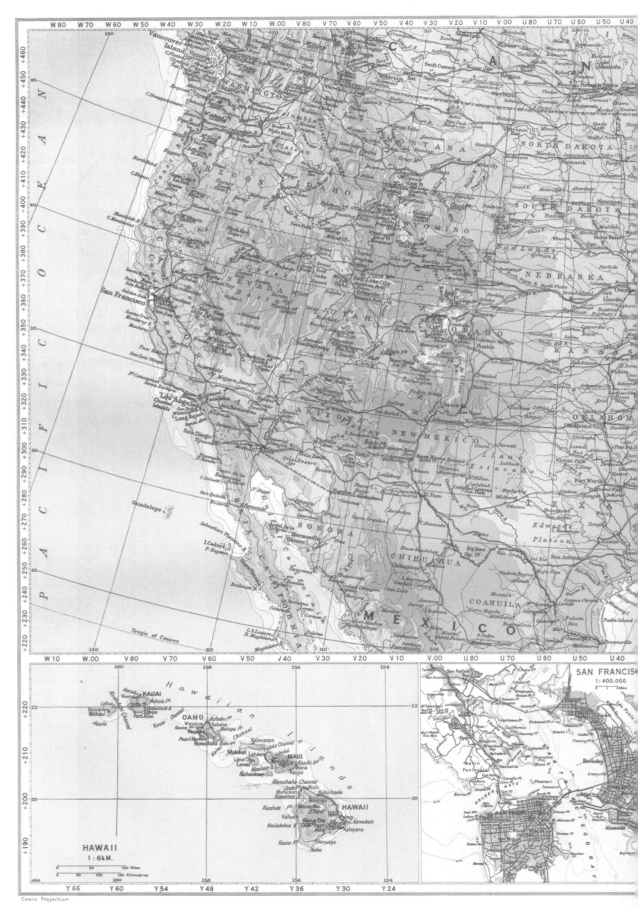

Free at Last? 1918–68

Part 1 – The USA in 1918

Part 2 – Jim Crow and the Ku Klux Klan

Part 3 – The civil rights campaigns between 1945 and 1965

Part 4 – Black Radical protest

Part 1 – The USA in 1918

In this section you will learn:
- Why thousands of immigrants arrived in the USA in the early twentieth century.
- Why attitudes towards immigrants changed in the early twentieth century.
- What was done to limit immigration to America in the 1920s.

The United States
in 1919
- southern states
- state borders
- US national border

At a glance:
Until the early twentieth century America had an 'open door' policy for immigrants, meaning that almost anyone could enter the country. Immigrants arrived in their millions, hoping to find 'the American Dream'. By 1919, for various reasons, America's 'open door' was closing and American policy towards immigrants was becoming more suspicious, resentful and racist.

What was an American in 1918?

One funny but often true definition of an American is 'somebody who came from somewhere else to become someone else'. In the early part of the twentieth century, most white 'Americans' were descendants of white Europeans who had arrived in the United States to escape from hardships at home and to search for a better standard of living.

Between 1901 and 1920, the population of the United States grew to over 105 million. During this time, almost 15 million new immigrants came to America. Almost 80% of this new wave of immigrants came from eastern and southern Europe.

By 1918 the USA was a multi-ethnic society. That means that people from all sorts of different cultures lived together in the USA. However, multi-ethnic does not mean that all racial groups were treated equally, or that they treated each other with respect.

What is the American Dream?

For many Americans, 'The American Dream' means the opportunity for anyone, regardless of their background, to become successful if they work hard. The American Dream also means equality of opportunity and the chance to 'make good'. A recent example of the American Dream is Barack Obama, who became president in 2008. His father came from a poor village in Kenya, and Barack Obama was brought up by his mother in Hawaii, an American state in the middle of the Pacific Ocean. All immigrants came to America hoping to find a better life, where they would be free and happy.

What were 'WASPs' and why did they think they were the most important group in America?

America has always been a land of immigrants. Until the middle of the nineteenth century, most immigrants came from northern Europe, in particular from Britain, Ireland, Germany and Scandinavia. Those 'older' immigrants took pride in how they had defeated the 'Red Indians' (now referred to as Native Americans) and made the USA a strong country. They said that the resources of the USA were gifts from God to be used to their advantage. They claimed it was their **manifest destiny** to develop the USA and keep it safe for their white, Anglo-Saxon, Protestant way of life.

By the end of the nineteenth century, most power in the USA was in the hands of these 'older' immigrants and a new nickname – WASP – was used to describe people descended from immigrants from northern Europe. WASP stands for White Anglo-Saxon Protestant. The immigrants who were descended from northern Europeans were obviously white, they came originally from a part of northern Europe that is described as Anglo-Saxon and they were mostly Protestant. Wealthier WASPs liked to think of themselves as the most powerful ethnic group in America.

What were 'new' immigrants and why did WASPs dislike them?

By the end of the nineteenth century, hundreds of thousands of immigrants were coming to the United States from poorer regions of Europe, for example, Italy, Poland and Russia. These 'new' immigrants left their homes to escape persecution and economic hardship in their homelands, and they believed that by working hard they could build new, better lives for themselves in America.

Many WASPs were afraid that the arrival of new immigrants from southern and eastern Europe threatened their way of life. Many of the new immigrants were Jewish or Catholic and looked very different from the more traditional immigrants from northern Europe. This fear of immigrants who were in some ways different from the the older WASP immigrants resulted in attacks on immigrants and new laws designed to restrict their entry into America.

Should black Americans be thought of as new immigrants to the USA?

No, they should not. Very few black people chose to emigrate to America in the early 1900s.

Most black Americans are descendants of Africans who were captured and taken to America as slaves over the last 400 years. For millions of black Americans living segregated lives, America in 1919 was not a free and equal land of opportunity.

In the southern states of the USA, black people were discriminated against by 'Jim Crow' laws and terrorised by the Ku Klux Klan. In the north, they suffered prejudice and discrimination. The experiences of black Americans are discussed in more depth on pages 78–80.

What happened to immigrants from Asia?

During the nineteenth century, many thousands of Chinese and Japanese had emigrated to America, many helping to build the railways. However, by 1900 the United States had already started to limit Asian immigration. The Chinese Exclusion Act of 1882 was the first important law restricting immigration into the United States. Chinese immigration to the United States was made illegal and by the early 1900s the United States was also starting to exclude Japanese immigrants.

What happened to Native Americans?

When the original European settlers arrived in America from Europe they did not find an empty land – it was already inhabited by millions of people, who were wrongly called 'Red Indians'.

By the middle of the nineteenth century, many hundreds of Native American tribes (known as nations) had been wiped out. The US government also had a policy of forcing Native Americans to live on small sections of poor-quality land called reservations, where they were barred from hunting and had to rely on government-issued food rations to survive.

In 1868, the US government had declared that all persons who were born in the USA or had become American were citizens of the United States.

However, the government soon ruled that Native Americans were not citizens and could not vote. By 1918, only small improvements in the lives of Native Americans had taken place. It was not until 1924 that Congress declared that all Native Americans born in the United States were citizens.

How did World War I affect attitudes towards immigration?

Between 1900 and 1914, millions of immigrants from the poorer areas of southern and central Europe flooded into America. When war broke out in Europe in 1914, that flood of immigrants was greatly reduced but when the war ended the US government feared that many more millions of immigrants would travel to America to start new lives.

During the war many Americans resented having to become involved in Europe's problems. After all, most of them had chosen to leave Europe's problems behind when they left for America. After the war the US government became isolationist. That meant they wanted nothing to do with any problems outside America. For that reason many US citizens did not want fresh waves of immigrants bringing 'European' problems to America.

Another issue concerned the use of propaganda in America during the war. A large part of the US immigrant population was of German or Austrian origin, but during the war the American public were persuaded that Germany was an enemy of America. Propaganda stories reported German atrocities during the war. Although some of those stories were made up, the public in America came to resent and dislike immigrants from Germany and the old Austrian Empire.

Why did Americans fear that immigrants might start a revolution?

In 1917, the Russian Revolution turned Russia into a communist state. Communism is a political ideology that is the exact opposite of the American political system. As many thousands of immigrants to the USA came from Russia and eastern Europe, the American authorities began to fear that the immigrants would bring communist ideas with them and perhaps start a revolution. That fear was called the 'red scare'. The word 'red' was used to mean communist.

The red scare was made worse by the terrorist activities of small revolutionary groups inside America who sent a number of bombs through the post to important Americans. American news stories were full of reports of how Mitchell Palmer, the top law enforcement officer in America, led raids to arrest suspected terrorists. When it became clear that there was no risk of revolution in America, the 'red scare' faded away – but not before it increased suspicion of immigrants.

How did immigrants make housing harder to find?

In the north-east of the USA, in and around New York, the large numbers of immigrants did make life harder for working-class Americans who already found their lives difficult enough.

Newly arrived immigrants needed somewhere to live. They tended to cluster in areas where other immigrants who shared the same culture had already settled. As a result, areas of north-eastern cities came to be known as Little Italy or Little Poland because of the people who settled there.

The great majority of new immigrants settled in cities where they could only afford to live in slum housing. The poor conditions in which they lived were a very serious problem for many immigrants. These slums became centres of disease and crime and they deteriorated further as more people, including the rural poor, arrived looking for cheap housing. Landlords knew that high demand meant they could raise rents without necessarily improving the quality of their housing. As a result, the WASP white working-class residents also saw their rents being forced up and housing harder to find as a result of immigration.

How did immigrants make jobs harder to find?

In the early 1900s, new ways of working in factories, which speeded up the production of many things, were being introduced. By using production line methods, the need for skilled workers was reduced. Factory owners realised they could make huge profits while at the same time employing immigrants and paying them rock-bottom wages. Suddenly, skilled workers in factories saw their jobs threatened by competition from new immigrants. Of course, it was not the fault of the immigrants, but nevertheless dislike of immigrants increased.

At the same time as immigration was increasing, trade union members were trying to get better wages and working conditions. When the union members campaigned for better conditions, for example, by going on strike, they found their bosses simply sacked them and replaced them with immigrants.

In the strikes which swept America in 1919, new immigrants were used as 'strike breakers'. Italian or Polish or Russian immigrants were prepared to work longer hours for lower wages than their American fellow workers. After all, they were still able to earn more than would have been possible back home in the 'old country'.

As the resentment towards immigrant strike breakers and rising rents increased, so did the desire to stop immigrants coming into the country.

How important was fear of crime in changing attitudes towards immigrants?

In the early 1920s, crime was increasing and many American politicians chose to blame immigrants. Crime had existed in America since its very beginning, and organised gangs had operated in New York and other cities for a long time. However, the newspapers of the time now had a new word to play with – Mafia! The Mafia is a name for organised crime gangs who originated in Sicily, in Italy. Naturally, as thousands of Italians emigrated to America, the Mafia became established there also.

Another development after World War I was increased dislike of both Italian and German immigrants. The US government believed that drinking alcohol was a bad thing so the Volstead Act of 1919 banned the sale of all alcohol. Banning the sale of alcohol is one thing, but it did not stop people wanting to drink it, so the organised crime gangs stepped in to supply the 'booze'. In the minds of the public, a strong connection was made between crime and the organised crime gangs of Italian immigrants.

A second connection was made between alcohol and immigrants. Many Germans were involved in the brewing industry (even today, Becks and Budweiser are popular brands that were originally made by German brewers) and if alcohol was a threat to the American way of life, then it stood to reason Germans were a bad influence too! Anti-immigration groups had many ways to stir up feeling against immigrants.

One case that shows how racism, fear of revolution and fear of crime all combined is the arrest and trial of two Italian-Americans called Nicola Sacco and Bartolomeo Vanzetti.

In 1920 Sacco and Vanzetti were accused of being involved in a robbery and murder. There is still considerable doubt over the two men's guilt and it is now generally believed that Sacco and Vanzetti were found guilty because of their political beliefs and where they came from.

After many appeals and a worldwide campaign to get the men released, Sacco and Vanzetti were executed by electric chair. It was clear that they had simply 'fitted the frame'. Sacco and Vanzetti were not recent immigrants but they had olive-coloured skin, were from Italian families and were anarchists. That meant they wanted to change the political system of America, possibly by violence. Finally, they were linked to 'Italian crime' so they were perfect targets for anti-immigrant prejudice.

Why did small-town America fear immigration?

New immigrants also faced prejudice and discrimination from Americans who saw them as a threat to 'the American way of life'. Those fears were most common in 'small-town America'.

Many Americans lived in small towns and communities that felt under threat. They felt their religious beliefs, their social customs and their democratic political system – in fact their whole way of life – was under threat from mass immigration.

'Nativism' is another word for small-town values, and was most common in the midwestern and southern states. In those 'Bible belt' areas, conservative ideas were popular. People there often believed that the Bible was literally true and that new ideas, even new scientific ideas such as evolution, were sinful. Nativists believed that immigrants brought new and sinful ideas into America, so they should be stopped from entering the country.

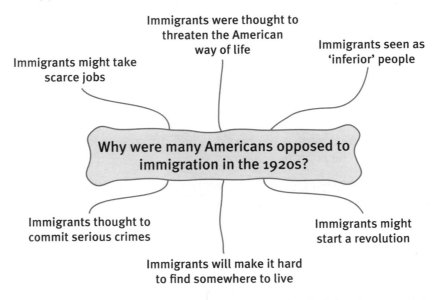

Immigrants were thought to threaten the American way of life

Immigrants might take scarce jobs

Immigrants seen as 'inferior' people

Why were many Americans opposed to immigration in the 1920s?

Immigrants thought to commit serious crimes

Immigrants might start a revolution

Immigrants will make it hard to find somewhere to live

Why did the Ku Klux Klan become very popular in the 1920s?

The Ku Klux Klan (KKK) was reinvented in 1915 as a direct response to growing fears of immigrants arriving with 'un-American' ideas. The original KKK was formed in the late 1860s and was known as an organisation that persecuted black Americans. However, from 1915 the KKK tapped into the fears of small-town America and declared it would protect white Anglo-Saxon Protestant Americans from Catholics, Jews and any foreign influence the Klan thought was 'un-American'. In fact, the new slogan of the Klan by 1920 was '100% American'. By the early 1920s the Ku Klux Klan was described as **the** social organisation for white, Protestant Americans. The WASPs welcomed the Klan into their churches, their homes and their lives. You can find out more about the Klan on pages 78–80.

How did America's open door for immigrants close in the 1920s?

Many Americans disliked the 'new' immigrants simply because they saw them as being different from themselves. By the early 1920s, there was clearly a very intolerant attitude towards new immigrants as they were blamed for many of the social problems of the time. As a result of growing public concern, US politicians began to campaign for immigration restrictions.

By 1921 the US government took its first steps towards closing the open door for immigrants.

A quota system only allowed a limited number of immigrants into the country. Every ten years most governments count how many people live in a country. That count is called a census. The US government knew from its 1910 census how many people of different nationalities lived in the USA. The government then announced that only 3% of each nationality already in the United States according to the 1910 census would be allowed to come into America. So, for example, if there had been 1000 people in America who had emigrated from Malta, then only a further 3% of this figure (in total thirty people) would be allowed into America from Malta.

The government soon realised it had made a mistake. By using the 1910 census it was accepting that many thousands of 'new' immigrants could get into the USA.

New restrictions in 1924 lowered the proportion from each country to 2%, based on the sizes of national groups in the United States at the time of the 1890 census – when there were far fewer 'new' immigrants living in the USA. By changing the rules the US government would not have to allow so many immigrants in from southern and central Europe!

Both the 1921 and the 1924 Immigration Acts discriminated unfairly against people who were not from western Europe. People from southern, central and eastern Europe found it harder to emigrate to America.

By 1929 it became even harder to gain entry to the USA. Only 150 000 immigrants a year were allowed to enter the United States and 85% of all places were reserved for immigrants from northern and western Europe. When President Coolidge declared that 'America must be kept American', he meant that the new immigration laws should limit the number of immigrants from southern and central Europe and allow in more from the traditional areas of northern and western Europe.

By 1930, immigration from southern and eastern Europe and Asia had almost stopped.

Part 2 – Jim Crow and the Ku Klux Klan

In this section you will learn:
- How Jim Crow laws made life difficult for black Americans.
- How the KKK used intimidation and fear to control black Americans in the southern states.
- Why nothing was done to stop the Jim Crow laws or the activities of the KKK in the 1920s and 1930s.

At a glance:

In 1918, most black Americans lived in the southern states of the USA. They often lived in poverty thanks to the sharecropping system. They were discriminated against by the Jim Crow laws and were terrorised by the Ku Klux Klan. Between 1900 and 1950, thousands of black Americans migrated to the northern cities to find a better life, but they still suffered discrimination and persecution.

Free at Last?

Why was there so much poverty among black Americans in the South.?

When slavery ended former slaves were free, but free to go where and do what? All they had known was farm work. From the plantation owner's point of view, they also had a problem. The owners of the plantations needed workers, lots of them. Now that slavery had been abolished, owners of plantations would have to pay wages but they could not afford to. Clearly, workers wanted work and plantation owners needed workers so the sharecropping system was adopted. Sharecropping meant that former slaves would be given plots of land to work and they would be given seeds and tools and machinery to farm their land **but not for free!**

At the end of the harvests, the workers would pay their debts by giving a share of their crop to the plantation owner who had given them the equipment. It meant that sharecroppers were always in debt so they were seldom free to leave their farms.

What were Jim Crow laws, and why did they make life so difficult for black Americans in the southern states?

Slavery was abolished by 1865 but the southern states used Jim Crow laws to maintain a segregated society in which white authority kept control over the black population. A segregated society means one in which people of a different colour are kept apart. 'Jim Crow' was a nickname for all sorts of laws that treated black Americans unfairly.

In the late nineteenth century, all of the southern states began to pass laws that reinforced white supremacy. These Jim Crow laws affected every part of a black American's life. Black children were forbidden to attend school with white children. Black Americans had only restricted access to public places such as parks and restaurants. At work they had separate bathrooms and collected their pay separately from whites. There were strict bans on whites and blacks marrying, and cemeteries even had to provide separate graveyards.

The situation was made even worse by a decision of the Supreme Court in 1896.

What did the Supreme Court decide in 1896?

The Supreme Court is the most important legal court in America. Its purpose is to make sure that no laws take away any of the basic human rights that are guaranteed in the American constitution. In 1896 the Supreme Court decided that segregation of black people from white people was acceptable, but was not meant to show that one race was better than another! Their ruling was called the 'separate but equal' decision. Basically the separate but equal decision accepted that Jim Crow laws were legal and acceptable across the USA. Mainly as a result of this ruling, segregation did not start to break down until 1954.

Could black Americans vote?

The answer is yes and no. Black men had been given the right to vote in 1870, but by 1900 almost no black person in the South was able to vote easily. To be able to vote in America it was necessary to register to vote, but many southern states created new voting rules specifically for black Americans that made it very difficult for them to register. Some examples of these voting qualifications included literacy tests, the ability to understand and explain complicated rules about the government and the introduction of a tax that had to be paid before registering to vote. Although there were areas, especially in the north, where black voters elected black representatives and senators, the reality was that most black Americans did not vote.

Partly as a result of the low numbers of black voters, politicians in the south needed to rely on the white voters. Since many of the white voters were also racist, it made no political sense to campaign to help black people in the south – or even to try to stop the torture and murder of black Americans that was known as lynching. Even Woodrow Wilson, who was president in 1918, described black Americans as 'an ignorant and inferior race'.

How important was the Ku Klux Klan in preventing progress towards civil rights?

The Ku Klux Klan was started in the late 1860s as a way of controlling newly freed slaves through fear. The Klan terrorised rural communities with night-time raids on black households. Black Americans in the southern states lived in fear of lynching. Lynching meant that a group of white people would capture and even murder a black person they believed was guilty of a crime. Victims were hanged and mutilated and their bodies sometimes burnt. The US government (also called the federal government) did almost nothing to stop lynching, and it was very difficult for black Americans to find justice in the south.

How did the KKK become such an important influence by 1918?

By the end of the nineteenth century the Klan seemed to have died away, but in 1915 it was re-formed and was helped hugely by a blockbuster movie called 'The Birth of a Nation'. The movie showed the Ku Klux Klan as protectors of southern white society against black terror. It was a phenomenal success, becoming the first film to make over $10 million, and the first movie to be shown in the White House.

Of course, the image of the Klan in the movie as heroic defenders of an American way of life was nonsense, but white Americans believed it. Black Americans knew that the Klan was an organisation that used fear and violence to deny black Americans their civil rights.

The new Klan claimed to be a patriotic organisation protecting the American way of life, devoted to '100% Americanism'. Klan members had to be native-born Americans, white and Protestant. There were even special Klan sections for women. The Klan attacked any group which it thought to be un-American. By the 1920s this included all non-Protestants, new immigrants and blacks.

How important was the Klan?

The Klan had friends in high places. In the 1920s, the Klan was powerful enough to hold large marches through Washington. Few Klansmen were arrested and in some communities local officials helped the Klan. In some state elections only candidates who were Klan-approved were allowed to stand for election. By the late 1920s, scandals involving sex and corruption had discredited the Klan but they still were (and remain even now) a symbol of white terror seeking to deny black Americans their civil rights.

What did black Americans do to try to improve their lives before 1945?

From 1918 onwards, many black Americans began a Great Migration north looking for better wages, better jobs and an escape from segregation and fear in the south. However, in the north thousands of poor white Americans were also looking for work and housing, and saw black Americans as unwelcome competition. Black people consequently found themselves segregated into communities and areas of cities known as ghettos. In 1919 there were several race riots in northern cities such as Washington and

Chicago. The riots were sparked off by racial tensions made worse by a lack of adequate housing. The Great Migration did help some black Americans to improve their lives. However, the bulk of black Americans lived in the southern states and their lives remained mostly unchanged. When World War II ended in 1945, the vast majority of black Americans still suffered as a result of prejudice, discrimination and fear.

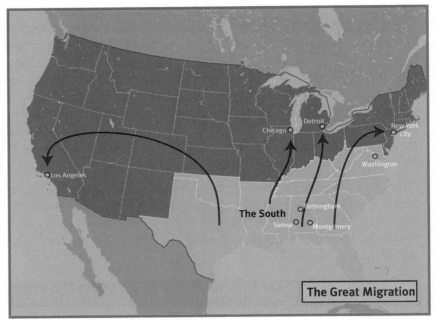

The Great Migration

Part 3 – The civil rights campaigns between 1945 and 1965

In this section you will learn:
- Why there was a growing demand for civil rights after 1945.
- How black Americans campaigned for civil rights in the 1950s and 1960s.
- How important Martin Luther King was to the civil rights movement.

At a glance:
After the end of World War II, growing demands for civil rights for black Americans swept across America. The main targets of the civil rights movement of the 1950s were segregation and the 'Jim Crow' laws. In the 1950s the civil rights movement campaigned mostly in the southern states of the USA. Those campaigns were influenced by the non-violent civil disobedience methods preached by Martin Luther King, Jnr. By the mid-1960s, new laws had been passed to enforce civil rights and make it easier for black Americans to vote. At the same time, some civil rights leaders argued that peaceful protest was not the way to change things in the northern cities. As a result, the civil rights campaign became split, and new leaders such as Malcolm X and Stokely Carmichael were prepared to use more violent protest methods.

What was the importance of World War II for black Americans?

Over a million black Americans fought for their country in World War II. They fought against Nazi aggression and racism yet they faced segregation and racism in their own army units and back home in the USA. As a result, many black soldiers began to talk of the 'double-V campaign'. The 'V' stood for victory in the war and victory for civil rights back home in the United States. However, little happened to change things until 1954.

Why was the decision of the Supreme Court in 1954 so important to civil rights?

The 1954 decision of the Supreme Court effectively overturned the 'separate but equal' decision of 1896. It showed that segregation was no longer acceptable in education, and this opened the doors to demands to end segregation everywhere.

In 1952, Oliver L. Brown from the city of Topeka, Kansas took the Topeka Board of Education to court over which school his daughter Linda could attend. Linda was black and so the local authority in the city of Topeka insisted that she attend a black school, even though the white schools were nearer and better equipped.

Mr Brown was supported in this action by a civil rights organisation called the National Association for the Advancement of Colored People. The NAACP aimed to achieve civil rights by working within the legal system. The NAACP saw the case of Linda Brown as an opportunity to attack segregation in education.

The case, which became known as Brown v. the Topeka Board of Education, ultimately reached the Supreme Court and in 1954 the Court declared that 'in the field of public education the doctrine of "separate but equal" has no place'. In effect, the Supreme Court reversed the 1896 decision by ruling that segregated schools did not have a place in modern America.

What caused the Montgomery Bus Boycott?

The bus boycott in Montgomery, Alabama was one of the first, and most important, protests in the campaign for civil rights, and had important results for the civil rights movement.

In December 1955, a black woman called Rosa Parks was arrested for refusing to give up her seat in a segregated city bus to a white man as the law demanded she should do. The NAACP had been waiting for just such an opportunity to launch a high profile campaign against Alabama's segregation laws.

The campaign took two forms. Firstly, the NAACP started a legal defence of Rosa Parks' actions in court.

Secondly, a bus boycott was started. For months, black Americans refused to use the buses in Montgomery and instead shared cars or simply walked in order to get about.

Was the Montgomery Bus Boycott important to civil rights?
On its own, the bus boycott only had limited success. It did not end all segregation and Montgomery remained a segregated town. However, the bus boycott showed what could be achieved by organised, peaceful, non-violent protest.

Martin Luther King, Jnr.

For the first time, black Americans realised that they had considerable economic power because they made up 60–70% of all bus passengers in Montgomery. The bus company realised that if it did not desegregate, it would go out of business.

Another big result of the bus boycott was the emergence of a new civil rights leader – Martin Luther King, Jnr.

What were the ideas of Martin Luther King?

When the bus boycott began in Montgomery, Alabama, Martin Luther King, had just started his first job as a church minister in that town. He was charismatic, and his ability to speak well soon put him at the front of the civil rights protests.

King put into words what so many black Americans had felt for so long. He said,

> **'There comes a time when people get tired – tired of being segregated and humiliated; tired of being kicked about by the brutal feet of oppression.'**

King believed that non-violent, peaceful civil disobedience was the best weapon in the fight for civil rights. King made it clear that he would not use violent force, saying 'in our protest there will be no cross burnings... there will be no threats or bullying'. He argued that it was the responsibility and the right of the citizens of a country to protest against a law that was wrong. In 1957, Martin Luther King, the Reverend Ralph Abernathy and others formed the Southern Christian Leadership Conference (SCLC) to campaign for civil rights.

What happened at Little Rock Central High School, Arkansas in 1957?

Many southern states attempted to ignore the Supreme Court's 1954 decision to end segregation in schools but in 1957, a federal court ordered that a group of nine black students be admitted to Little Rock's Central High School in the state of Arkansas. When the Arkansas National Guard (a sort of local army) prevented the black students from entering the all-white school, US President Eisenhower eventually sent 1000 federal troops to Little Rock to protect the black students.

Why did events at Little Rock Central High School, Arkansas in 1957 affect civil rights?
By the mid-1950s, most American homes had television. For the first time people could see what was happening in places such as Little Rock. The world was shocked when one black student called Elizabeth Eckford turned up for school and was met by a mob that wanted to kill her.

The late 1950s was also a time when America claimed it was the home of freedom. When film of Elizabeth Eckford being bullied and threatened just for attending a white school was shown around the world, Russia, who was America's enemy at the time, used those images to claim that America was very far from being a land of the free. President Eisenhower was embarrassed. Something had to be done.

What were sit-ins?

On 1 February 1960, four black students sat down and attempted to order some food at a whites-only lunch counter in Greensboro, North Carolina. They were refused service but remained in their seats until closing time. They returned the following day with twenty-five supporters who continued the sit-in. By 5 February there were more than 300 students, black and white, taking part in the protest.

TV news showed local white youths attacking the demonstrators, but when the police arrived it was the demonstrators who were arrested. The problem was that as soon as demonstrators were carried away from the lunch counters more demonstrators took their place. The police, the jails and the courts all over the South were being overwhelmed by the campaign to fill the jails.

By the end of the year, more than 700 000 protestors had participated in sit-ins across the country. Although thousands of the students were arrested and physically assaulted, they refused to retaliate, and followed the ideas of non-violent protest.

How successful were the sit-ins?
In many ways, the sit-ins were highly successful. National television coverage highlighted the violent racist reaction of many southerners, whilst the courage, commitment and sacrifice of the demonstrators won them support across the country. By the summer of 1960, many lunch counters in the south had been desegregated.

However, the sit-ins did not end all segregation in the South, and their impact was only really felt at a local level.

What were the Freedom Rides?

In May 1961, the Congress of Racial Equality (CORE) sent a group of 'freedom riders' to challenge the south's Jim Crow laws. Along with CORE members were members of the Student Non-violent Coordinating Committee (SNCC). Black students created this organisation in April 1960 to help coordinate, support and publicise the sit-in campaign.

The plan was to travel south on interstate buses. Interstate highways (like motorways) and the service area rest rooms were the responsibility of the national federal authority, not state authority. In areas under federal authority there should have been no segregation. The freedom riders wanted to see if segregation in interstate public facilities had really ended.

The freedom riders expected a violent reaction from the southern racists but they stuck to their belief in non-violent protest. Their plan was to seat blacks and whites together on the buses, a crime in many cities. They also intended to send black students into 'white only' rest rooms and for white students to use 'colored only' rooms. At first, they met with little resistance, but as they travelled south, bus tyres were slashed, buses were firebombed and the freedom riders were beaten up.

Did the freedom rides help to gain civil rights?
Once again the TV news coverage deeply shocked the American public. Martin Luther King attempted to persuade the riders to stop for fear that they would be killed, but the freedom rides continued throughout the summer – as did the violence. In late 1961, the federal government finally ordered an end to all segregation in airports and rail and bus stations.

Why were events in Birmingham, Alabama so important to civil rights?

In 1963, the civil rights movement turned its attention to Birmingham, Alabama – a city that Martin Luther King had described as being the most segregated city in America. King said the campaign in Birmingham would be the toughest fight of the civil rights campaign. George Wallace, the new governor of Alabama, was totally opposed to the civil rights movement and famously proclaimed: 'Segregation now, segregation tomorrow, segregation forever.'

At first the demonstrations achieved little publicity. As the weeks dragged on, demonstrators felt they were achieving little. When they were arrested they lost their jobs and their pay packets. Support for the demonstrations was falling away when King decided on a risky strategy. He knew the police chief in Birmingham was an extreme racist called Eugene 'Bull' Connor. King knew that if he could provoke Bull Connor, the cameras would show images that would shock the world.

On 2 May 1963, another demonstration was organised, this time involving over 1000 schoolchildren. At first the children were just arrested but, as the city's jails filled to bursting, Bull Connor tried another means of preventing the demonstration. He called out the fire department and the police dogs.

American people watched their televisions in shock and disbelief as white officers savagely attacked schoolchildren as young as eight, first with powerful fire hoses and then with tear gas, dogs and even electric cattle prods.

Free at Last?

How important was the effective use of media such as TV in gaining support for civil rights?

Martin Luther King's tactics were risky, but they worked. King and other young black leaders realised the importance of television and the media. They hoped that film of white racists attacking black Americans in public would force the US government to take action. The events in Birmingham caused an outcry across America and throughout the world, causing public opinion to swing behind the civil rights campaign. President Kennedy was forced to order an end to all segregation in Birmingham. Once again, it had become necessary for the federal government to intervene in order to force a state government to obey federal law.

How important was the march on Washington in August 1963?

On 28 August 1963, over 200 000 blacks and whites marched towards the Lincoln Memorial in Washington, DC. The huge gathering of demonstrators was not designed to gain anything other than publicity, which it achieved brilliantly. It was the largest civil rights demonstration in American history, and four national television channels broadcast the event live. The speech that Martin Luther King gave has become known as the 'I have a dream' speech and is considered to be one of the most famous and important speeches of the twentieth century.

How important was the Civil Rights Act of 1964?

The 1964 Act did a great deal to end discrimination and segregation and declared that:
- racial discrimination in any public place in the United States, such as petrol stations, restaurants, hotels and movie theatres, was banned
- discrimination on the basis of race, religion, national origin or sex was banned in any place employing more than twenty-five people
- any state government that still discriminated against black Americans would face charges in a federal court.

On the other hand, the new law did nothing to solve discrimination in housing or give black people a fair and free vote.

The Act did not end fear and discrimination. The KKK still used terror against any black person who tried to use the freedoms that the Act was supposed to guarantee.

However, most people agreed that the Civil Rights Act was a big move towards helping black Americans achieve full civil rights.

When commenting on the Civil Rights Act of 1964, Martin Luther King said that it 'gave Negroes some part of their rightful dignity, but without the vote it was dignity without strength'.

How did black Americans gain the right to vote freely?

In order to cast a vote, voters first of all had to register. Black Americans had gained the right to vote many years before, but throughout the south, difficulties in registering to vote still prevented many black Americans from casting their votes.

In March 1965, King led a march from Selma to Birmingham, Alabama to publicise the way authorities in the south made it difficult for black Americans to vote.

The campaign leaders knew that violent white resistance would meet the march. Publicity had worked in Birmingham, so why not in Selma?

Predictably, when the march began, the Alabama authorities tried to stop it with tear gas and mounted police. Television coverage of the march and the attack caused national anger and prompted President Johnson to provide National Guardsmen to protect the marchers.

Was the Selma to Montgomery march a success?

In August 1965, Congress passed the Voting Rights Act which removed the various barriers to registration – such as the requirement to reable to read and write – that had been used to stop black Americans voting. By the end of the year, over 250 000 black Americans were newly registered.

The Voting Rights Act marked the end of the civil rights campaigns in the south. By 1965, the focus of civil rights protests had moved north, and the style of protest had changed.

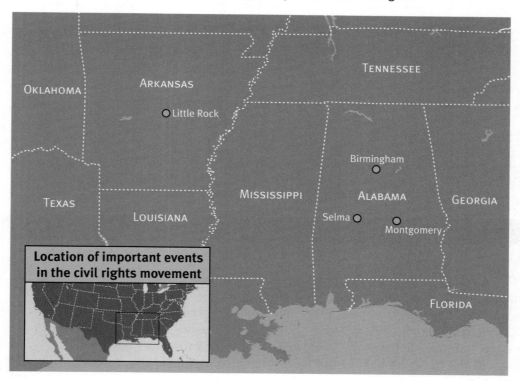

Part 4 – Black Radical protest

In this section you will learn:
- The ways in which civil rights protests changed in the 1960s.
- What the ideas of Stokely Carmichael and Malcolm X were.
- How successful the Black Radical protests of the late 1960s were.

At a glance:

Not all black leaders supported King's policy of non-violence. Stokely Carmichael started to speak about 'Black Power', and both he and Malcolm X rejected white help. More and more the earlier campaigns for voting rights and desegregation were criticised as being irrelevant to the needs of urban black Americans in the cities of the north and west.

By the late 1960s, urban race riots and new organisations such as the Black Panthers and the Nation of Islam had grabbed the headlines. The new groups who used violent direct action in their protests were called collectively Black Radicals. The Black Radical groups wanted improvements in housing, education and employment opportunities. They also argued that black Americans should be prepared to defend themselves and fight back, using violence if necessary. Non-violent protest was rejected as a failure.

When and how did the civil rights movement split?

The split in the civil rights movement became obvious during the March against Fear in 1966.

Stokely Carmichael

While King and his supporters chanted 'freedom now' and encouraged white Americans to join the march, a new, more militant leader of the SNCC called Stokely Carmichael chanted 'Black Power' and rejected white help. The split in the civil rights movement was made more obvious when the SNCC changed the meaning of the 'N' in its name from 'non-violent' to 'national'. By the mid 1960s, many black Americans no longer believed that non-violence was the way forward.

What was Black Power?

The main ideas of Black Power were:
- black Americans should not rely on white people to 'give' them civil rights;
- white support for the civil rights movement was not wanted;
- black Americans should build up their own schools, communities, businesses, even hospitals, without interference from whites.

Many young black Americans living in the urban ghettos were attracted to the Black Power movement by Stokely Carmichael's more extreme, aggressive message, summed up when Carmichael said 'I am not going to beg the white man for anything I deserve. I'm going to take it.'

On the other hand, Carmichael put an emphasis on racial pride and raising black consciousness with his much-repeated phrase, 'black is beautiful'. He also said that 'Black Power' simply meant fulfilling the aim of getting black Americans to control their own political and economic futures. He wanted separate black political parties, black-owned businesses and independent schools for black Americans.

By 1966, the idea of Black Power had become established as an alternative to King's non-violent protest methods.

What were the beliefs of the Nation of Islam?

Another black radical group that gained popularity with urban black Americans was the Nation of Islam. The Nation of Islam was founded in Detroit in 1930. It supported the creation of a separate black nation on the US mainland, separate from white society in every way – economically, politically and spiritually.

The Nation of Islam attracted many with its ideas of strict moral discipline and religious observance, and its apparent ability to 'straighten out' the lives of many individuals such as drug addicts and criminals who had been considered beyond hope. One of those 'saved' souls was Malcolm X.

Who was Malcolm X?

Malcolm Little was a small-time criminal who was converted to a version of the Islamic faith while in jail. It was called the Nation of Islam, or more commonly the black Muslims, and was led by Elijah Muhammad. Malcolm Little changed his name to Malcolm X. He claimed that his surname was a white name given to his family by slave owners many years before, so the 'X' referred to his unknown African name. Until he and his followers rediscovered their African names they would use letters as their last names, representing their stolen identities.

Malcolm X became a minister for the Nation of Islam and was one of the most charismatic and articulate opponents of King's belief in non-violence.

Malcolm X did not support integration (the mixing of races – the opposite of segregation), and argued that black Americans should develop their society to be separate from whites. Unlike King, who believed in the American Dream, Malcolm X saw an 'American Nightmare'. Malcolm X was one of the first black activists to draw attention to the increasing urban problems within the ghettos of American cities – crime, prostitution, drugs and unemployment.

He believed that white society was corrupt and racist, and that America's claim to be a land of the free was false and applied only to white people. He rejected help from whites and stated that black Americans needed to work out their own futures without relying on white help.

Malcolm X declared that non-violence was another word for being defenceless and he clearly rejected the aims and methods of Martin Luther King. Malcolm X's message of self-help attracted many listeners tired of having to wait on white authority to improve conditions.

He warned that if nothing was done, violence would erupt.

Why was Malcolm X assassinated?

Malcolm X split with the Nation of Islam in 1963 after an argument with its leader, Elijah Muhammad. Malcolm X also changed his mind about white people after a visit to Africa and the Middle East. He wrote that some whites were sincere and that black and white people could work together. He also described Elijah Muhammad as a 'racist and a faker'. Probably as a result of his falling out with Elijah Muhammad, Malcolm X's home was firebombed and a week later he was murdered while giving a speech. The three gunmen were linked to the Nation of Islam. It was February 1965.

Why did riots break out in so many cities during the 1960s?

By 1965, half of all black Americans lived in the cities of the north and west. Most of them lived in slum areas that were known as ghettos. They had to live with bad housing, high rents, unemployment, poverty and hunger. Urban gang violence and drug-associated crime were also increasing. One teenager summed up the problem of the ghetto when he said,

> **'In the ghettos the white man has only one handicap: he is poor. The black man has two handicaps. He is poor and he is black.'**

In 1965, the Watts district of Los Angeles was 98% black, but the police force was almost entirely white. The combination of a long, hot summer, poverty, unemployment and violent police action sparked off a riot that lasted for 6 days and left 34 dead, 900 wounded and 4000 arrested. To restore order, 14 000 troops were required, but not one of the causes of the riot was dealt with.

The importance of the Watts Riot, and others which followed, was to show that economic and social issues were far more important to black people in the cities than the 'older' civil rights issues of desegregation and voting rights in the South.

For many young, black Americans in the cities, the civil rights movement of the 1950s and early 1960s was an irrelevance. The protestors in the cities agreed that they could ride on the same buses, eat in the same restaurants and even live in the same districts as white people but, without jobs and money, what real benefits had the civil rights campaign brought them?

How did Martin Luther King try to continue his style of protest in the northern cities?

King was aware of the growing Black Radical protests and the discontent in the urban ghettos. He knew he had to deliver improvements in those areas if he was to retain support for his style of civil rights campaigning. He was well aware that he was no longer headline news and television reporting focused more and more on the extremist statements of the Black Radical groups.

King and the SCLC were worried that the increasing use of violent protest methods by the radical groups would lose public and federal support in America.

However, King and his followers realised that if they did nothing, leadership of the civil rights movement would fall into the hands of the more violent and militant protesters. As a result, King and his followers moved north to attack the problems of the cities.

Not everyone welcomed King's move. Some opponents said that city problems were just too big for Martin Luther King's style of campaign. In some cities, such as New York and Philadelphia, black leaders even asked King not to go near them. Chicago, however, invited King to help.

Did Martin Luther King fail in Chicago?

Urban riots in 1965 convinced King that Chicago had become the symbol of the race problem in northern cities. King believed that if he could make a difference there, his support would revive. King selected segregated housing as the main issue for his protest to focus on.

King hoped to use similar tactics to those he had used in the south. By targeting one area and one issue, he hoped to provoke a showdown, gain media sympathy and thereby win his case.

Unfortunately for King, Chicago was not a southern town. The mayor of Chicago was Richard Daley, a powerful politician who knew how to handle the media and how to cope with opposition to his policies.

King arranged a protest march through an area of Chicago surrounded by several white working-class neighbourhoods, but the march failed. Mayor Daley made some vague promises to King about improvements in housing but these promises were not kept. Far from restoring his credibility in the civil rights campaign, the Chicago protest weakened Martin Luther King's influence. Many people were more attracted to calls for Black Power.

Did the assassination of Martin Luther King mark the end of the civil rights campaigns?

King knew his influence was slipping away. Despite the increasing pressure to change his ideas to attract new support, King stuck to what he believed in. He intended to show America that he could still use non-violent protest to improve people's lives.

In the spring of 1968, King went to Memphis, Tennessee, to support a strike by rubbish collectors over equal pay for black workers. The first march had ended in violence, and the night before the next protest march he seemed to foresee his own death. He said,

> **'Like anybody, I would like to live a long life but I'm not concerned about that now. I may not get there with you. But I want you to know tonight, that we, as a people, will get to the Promised Land.'**

On 4 April 1968, Martin Luther King was shot and killed as he stood on his motel balcony in Memphis, Tennessee.

When word spread of his death, riots erupted in 168 cities. To restore order, 70 000 American troops were needed. It seemed that the non-violent civil rights movement had died with King.

What did Martin Luther King achieve?

Martin Luther King was a charismatic leader who knew how to use the relatively new medium of television to gain public sympathy and to pressurise federal authority. He helped make changes so that life in America, especially in the south, was very different in 1965 to what it had been in 1955.

Even Stokely Carmichael said that Martin Luther King was the one man whom the masses of black Americans would listen to. Nearly every black American, and most whites, agree that Martin Luther King was one of the most important leaders of any colour in the twentieth century. He remains an icon representing dignified protest against unjust conditions and unfair treatment of human beings.

How did the Black Panthers represent the new style of Black Radical protest?

By the late 1960s, a new group – the Black Panthers – grabbed the headlines as one of the most radical protest groups.

The Black Panther Party for Self-Defence was founded in October 1966 in Oakland, California by Huey P. Newton and Bobby Seale. The Black Panthers represented the complete opposite of Martin Luther King's ideas and supported the anti-white, black separatist ideas of Stokely Carmichael and Malcolm X. The Panthers were prepared to use violence in order to achieve their goals and saw the police as the enemy of black communities.

Although the Black Panthers gained publicity because of their threatening image (wearing black leather jackets, black berets, dark glasses and carrying guns) they were also involved in self-help schemes inside the urban ghettos. They organised community programmes such as free breakfasts for children, free health clinics and campaigns to stop drugs and crime in black areas of American cities.

In their ten-point programme, the Black Panthers echoed many of the complaints of America's black urban population. Their demands included full employment for all, better housing that was 'fit for the shelter of human beings', honest education, an end to police brutality and fair trials with black juries for black people.

How important were the Black Panthers?

The deliberately threatening poses used in the self-publicity of the Black Panthers grabbed headlines at a time when much of white society was afraid of black protest movements. However, it would be wrong to think that most black Americans were prepared to use violent tactics to improve civil rights. Only a small number were willing to use the violence that the Black Panthers proposed, and even at their height the Black Panthers only had 2 000 members.

What did the Kerner Commission's report say about civil rights in America?

This topic is called **Free at Last?** and ends in 1968. The question mark in the title is important. The title is not stating that black Americans were free at last in 1968. It is asking to what extent were black Americans free by 1968. In other words, how successful had the civil rights campaigns been up until that date?

In 1968 King was dead. The year before King's death, one of the most destructive riots had taken place in Detroit. Several people were killed and millions of dollars' worth of property was destroyed.

After the Detroit riot, President Johnson asked Otto Kerner to lead a commission to investigate thoroughly the causes of the urban riots. President Johnson suspected that a minority of people were using the urban problems as an excuse to start a revolution in America. He did not believe the riots were a genuine reaction of people who felt they had no other options but to riot.

When the Kerner Commission made its report public in 1968, Americans were shocked by what it said.
- America was divided into two societies – one black and poor, the other white and richer
- 40% of all black Americans lived in poverty
- black men were twice as likely to be unemployed as white men
- black men were three times as likely to be in low-skilled jobs
- the riots and other crimes were caused by poverty

The Kerner Commission concluded that

> **'our nation is moving towards two societies, one black, one white – separate and unequal'.**

It went on to say that,

> **'What white Americans have never understood – but what the Negro can never forget – is that white society is deeply implicated in the ghetto. White institutions created it, white institutions maintain it, and white society condones it.'**

In other words, the problems of the urban ghettos were not caused by outside troublemakers. The problems of the ghettos were caused by genuine poverty that was the result of the lack of opportunities for black Americans to improve their lives.

The Kerner Commission's report would be very useful to use in any answer about the success, or otherwise, of the civil rights campaign up to 1968. You have two very usable quotes from it provided for you here. Perhaps they could feature in a conclusion to your work.

The Kerner Commission's report reminded America that it was still a long way from being a free and equal society. The world was reminded of the civil rights issue at the 1968 Mexico Olympics, when two black American runners mounted the rostrum to receive their medals. As the Stars and Stripes flag rose and the American national anthem played, the athletes raised clenched fist salutes and bowed their heads. The world could see that Black Power was still alive in the United States and that racial tension still existed.